DAY TRADING

Day Trading Strategies For Beginners, Options
For A Living, And Swing Options

MARK REESE

Table of Contents

Introduction

Day trading describes as buying and selling a security within one day of trading. To benefit minor price changes in highly volatile stocks or currencies, they use significant levels of leverage and short-term trading strategies.

Day traders geared to activities that trigger market fluctuations in the short term. News-trading is a common technique. Scheduled reports are subject to consumer perceptions and market dynamics, such as economic indicators, company earnings, or interest rates. Markets respond when those expectations are not met or surpassed, usually with major, rapid moves that can help day traders.

A controversial activity, perhaps one of the most misunderstood subjects on Wall Street, is the benefits potential of day trading. Internet day trading scams have tempted amateurs to offer significant returns in a short period. The belief remains that this sort of trading is a get-rich-quick scheme. Without proper information, some people trade day in. Yet there are day traders who, despite —or maybe because of— the risks, make a good living.

Most experienced fund managers and financial planners shy away from day trading, believing that the gain isn't worth the risk in most situations. Those who do day-trade, on the other hand, insist there is a profit to make. Day trading is lucrative, but ultimately the performance rate is lower due to the difficulty and required risk of day trading in combination with the associated scams.

Day trading is not for everyone and entails significant risks. It includes an in-depth understanding of how the markets operate and various short-term benefit strategies. Although you remember those who struck it rich as a day trader's success, stories note that most don't — many are going to fizzle out, and others are just barely going to remain afloat. Also, don't underestimate the role that chance and good timing play—whereas ability is an aspect, even the most experienced day trader can sink a rout of lousy luck.

Let's first be specific on what day-trading isn't. It's not saving, which is the process of purchasing a share in an asset, which will ideally create a long-term profit. How long is subjective, but for years' investors usually keep money, even decades. So they generally concern themselves with the undertakings they participate in and are searching for businesses that make good money, pay off debts on time, have a compelling product pipeline, and escape lawsuits.

On the other hand, day-trading entails buying and selling shares within the same day. Day traders also use borrowed money in highly traded stocks or indices to take advantage of the minor price fluctuations. They usually adopt the same philosophy as long-term investors: they seek to buy low and sell high in a somewhat short period.

If the benefit from the trader looks like small potatoes, note that day traders do not make one or two trades a day — they can make 25 to 30. Their gains thus compounded by increasing the number of trades.

In general, day traders won't buy stock overnight to reduce their risks because rates can shift dramatically from one day to the following. News events and corporate announcements also trigger the market volatility, so traders have to be accessible and ready to respond at a time notice. Day traders act rapidly, making decisions in minutes, even seconds, unlike investors who may wait until rationality prevails or until additional information becomes available.

CHAPTER 1:

How to Start Trading

D ay trading is becoming a lucrative engagement in the commerce industry with recent technological advancement. Hey there, welcome to the stock market world. This end is strategically oriented and plenty of significant risks coming your way. Let's dive into some of the factors that are likely to be considered.

The Capital Needed to Start Day Trading

Capital is so necessary to set the actual day trading ball on fire. Acquiring loans from different sites has been revealed to be so common among traders. With this glue on the mind, traders tend to be so careful with the amount of capital that they intend to commence. Traders ought to obtain ready money to monitor any kind of slight changes that are presumed to occur during the day.

Day trading requires a minimum account balance of $1000, but many providers and plenty of traders recommend $10,000 are not willing to risk 1% from the value. Also, the $1000 minimum amount that can implement can lead to your trading activities in being so not worthwhile.

Step by step kind of beginning is so vital because you get to acquire progress always and get to grow at a reasonable speed with messing things out.

Choosing a Broker

Once you have set your mind on precisely what intend to trade, a broker should be following up in mind. Brokers are the navigators of several trading investment platforms. Bearing this I mind, we ought to be super perfect in choosing a broker because they reflect reliability, reputations, and expertise in your trading account.

Let us look at some of the ways that set to consider:

- **Decide On What You Will Be Trading**

Experts get their names by being suitable (perfect) in a particular field of trading. A stocks broker may be so bad in FOREX trading and vice versa—all the best in picking the best and the right one.

- **Sourcing for Recommendations**

Sticking in mind that the actual amount of money to be used during trading is your own money, a wake-up call is assured, and a good broker who can't be dodging with your precious money is super needed.

Try to inquire your colleagues if you may have been in a spot or who they may have heard of good brokers. Try to also have some in-depth research from varieties of social media content, online on the investment platforms, discussion boards and also take plenty of time to examine their websites.

Once you get several references, don't hesitate to check on their trading platforms. How were their actions? Are there complaints? How many traders have they ever engaged? How long have they been doing this? Have they been following the rules and regulations needed as a broker?

- **Commission Rate**

Although the "perfect" broker is super needed as you begin day trading, consider in mind that this is also a new project as a whole. Consider the rates of commissions that are likely to be spent to avoid any losses from being made. Pick an economical one to save yourself.

- **Executive Speed**

Any delay of seconds can result in a massacre to a trader's profits. To prevent this, the broker should make sure that the trading activities are at a top-notch. The broker should be able to quickly spot any rapid changes that are likely to be incurred in the trading platforms.

- **Charting Strategies**

Getting great chatting tools and software is also fundamental. Make sure you are getting right trading strategies, reliable variable markets, and better software features to enhance good day trading

- **Paper Trading**

It's advisable to begin day trading with paper trading, where you won't have to use your own money, though many brokers highly discourage this. Know where your heart takes you.

- **Technology**

So, is the broker up for the new technological advancements? What kinds of accounts do they deal? Does he/she have a real-time-data feed so that you can easily track and monitor trading activities? Which safeguard trading and Cybersecurity measures do they follow during trading? What kind of volumes of trading can they handle?

Much consider the kind update with the current technological happenings and pretty much informed.

- **Customer Service Provision**

Are they willing to offer customer service services? What happens when your system during mid-trade and it costs you so much? Are they going to support you to get much out of trading? Which process are they going to utilize during complaint resolution? Consider these before signing the contract because it's a big deal.

- **Safe, Secure and Regulated**

It's such a marvelous idea to inquire about the security of the broker in question. Inquire on how long they have been in business, their past work reports, what measures they have been using and their new significant standards on day trading.

Make sure they regulated by an agency and that they strictly value and consider the rules and regulations needed to be followed by any broker engaged in day trading.

- **Adequate Support**

Engage with brokers that are willing to provide massive support once there is a miss during your daily training activities. A few cents incremented on the broker's commission accounts is much worthwhile compared to hundreds of dollars' losses that are likely to be incurred on the bad days.

Type of Market

Each kind of day trading demands a different type of day trading. Choosing the type of market to start with is super important, choose the most preferred.

Discover the tax implications likely to be incurred.

Inquire on how taxes revolve around profits. Engage with your financial adviser to let him or her explain how taxes handled. Are they going to cause devaluation on the made profits? Are they good news? How does that happen?

Be informed to at the end the trader can guess on the likelihood net profits to be expected. Set a target, really motivating.

Setting a realistic trading target is going to manage and monitor your real cash big time. A specific goal put for big motivation. Work on that. Be for it big time. Remember achieving your target usually is tough because we all have really "dream" targets. Consistent losses will incur too, so prepare to lose some cash. Failure is never right though and will never be, so keep up champ!

Create a Demo Account

Rehearsing has always been a good move as your head to be successful navigation. Set up a demo account that will help you master all the ropes and movements that are likely to be incurred. The market trends are one way of future taking master moves that are great chances for high profitability rates. Keep testing and practicing until you are sure that you indeed set to go. Examine the market.

Master most of the trading moves. It makes you informed and enhances specialization in a particular field.

Fast Internet Connection

A constant, fast and reliable type of internet connection recommended. The unreliable internet connection can cause a miss in the market trends that can hinder the trading traces in a way leading to significant losses incurred at the end. Most of the users use a cable and ADSL type of connection. Remember that day trading does not recommend any unreliable source of contact.

Choose the Right Stocks to Trade

Well, to be better in choosing the right kind of stock, doing some in-depth research on the current existing stock is way the first step. Get to know the type of stocks that are likely to perform well. Most preferably those are likely to achieve well on a day-to-day basis. Remember to at least try one or two different kinds of stock until you are so sure that you have picked out the right one.

Plan a Notable Financial Figure

You will need to prepare yourself early enough on the amount of money that risked on the day trading business. It is mostly advised not to risk more than 1-2% of your account money to avoid future losses.

Another piece of advice to the beginners, stay away from trading on the margin until you set with enough moves and sound trading wisdom. It will save you some extra cash in time.

Venture into several day trading courses to get educated.

Before getting involved in a particular course of study, kindly consider the following tips:

- **The course should be taught by a professional**

You can acquire detailed, accurate, reliable, and up to date information. It will so motivate you in your trading journey.

- **Availability of educational support tools**

The presence of proper educational tools will give the learner an audience to readily grasp every fundamental piece of information. The professional should also be ready to face time or live chat with any student who needs excellent help.

- **Based on your particular field**

Well, we agreed on picking out a particular trading sector field and working on it. Well, your educational source should go hand in hand in whatever area that you have selected. Make sure that the learning source is detailed to acquire a more significant piece of information.

- **High rated learning the source**

A perfectly detailed piece of learning information entails that a lot has covered. Go for that. We have to make our day trading journeys so well, and then meaning that our start-off spots should be right.

Putting all these in mind, take a look at some excellent sources for beginners:

- Books and journals

- Online courses for day trading

- Applications for games

- Beginner level books for day trading

Perform a Personal Audit

Day trading is much of analytical work. A clear understanding of what is going to take place is so needed. Day trading is not a get-rich-overnight thing. It's a step by step learning project that involves simple to sophisticated tactics that get to be implemented by the trader during his/her day trading journey.

Set The Right Strategies

First things first, getting to know what you are working on is an essential activity. What do I want? How are you going to achieve all these? Is it worth it? How long is this going to take? What are the possible outcomes?

A little reminder, a proper strategically outline calls for hard work and patience to achieve a singular goal.

CHAPTER 2:

How to Read the Main Tools and Charts

One thing to always remember is - the charts don't lie. The charts represent the money on the table at the end of the day. That is why they are of significant importance.

Charts are a widely used tool in trading and investing to see the past performance of the stock quickly, the highs, the lows, trends, moving averages, trading volume, and much more.

Charts really are the "footprint of money." What some talking head on a financial news network might say becomes immaterial when you can look at a chart and see what the 'money' is saying. That's what is essential. Seeing the money on the table and understanding by the propensity of evidence who was buying and selling and how serious they were.

Charts in Detail

We will start with a single Line Chart and Bar Chart and progress from there.

A line connecting following closing prices is the purest form of charting. These line charts are useful for trend analysis going back 2 – 5, or even 10 years or more.

See Figure 3 below:

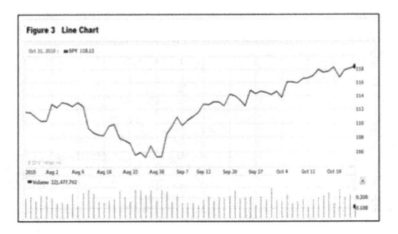

The chart below is a bar chart and is one of the most basic forms of charting. Even in its simplicity, we can determine the general movement of the stock, and draw a reasonable conclusion as to the possibility of future movement.

See Figure 3-2 below:

As you can see, the stock was trading in December (center of the chart) in the $35 to $40 range and over the course of 6- months it doubled in price. This was obviously during the tech boom of the late 90s or early 2000. Thus, over a 6-month period of time, the primary trend was up.

Note that each day in the above chart is indicated by a separate 'bar.' Each bar has a little 'tick' on the left side indicating the opening price that day, and the little 'tick' on the right side of the bar indicated the closing price for that day. The length of the bar tells us the trading range for that particular day, as noted by the arrows on the above chart. Here is a closer look at how the daily bars on a chart indicate the opening price, the closing price, and the trading range for the day.

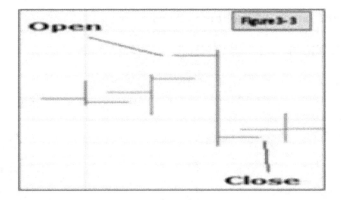

Remember this as we progress.

Also remember that whether you are looking at a daily, hourly, or even a weekly chart, the trends and pattern formations will tell you pretty much the same thing in relation to the chart you are viewing. Meaning, if you are looking at a daily chart, then the general trend should be viewed as a daily basis. In other words, do not make decisions for long-term investments based on what you see on a 5-minute chart or an hourly chart. And don't make day-trading decisions based solely on a one-year chart.

For instance: A 3-month chart shows the daily bars for each trading day represented on that chart. And, a chart of one single trading day will show 1-minute, 5-minute, or possibly 10-minute bars. But each bar represents its open, close, and the trading range for its respective time period.

The construction of a daily bar chart is simple. Fortunately, these are free on the Internet and constructed for you. The vertical bar is drawn from the day's high to the low. The tick to the left is the opening price that day; the tick to the right is the closing price.

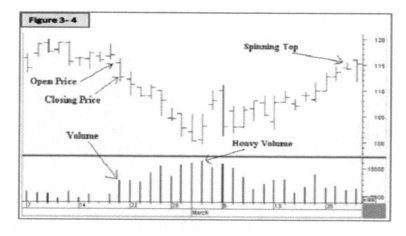

Figure 3-4

Volume bars are drawn along the bottom of the chart. See these indicated by the arrows on the above chart.

These are constructed for you, but it is vitally important that you understand what each bar and their several ticks mean. These will be used in detail as we progress.

Candlestick Style Chart

Another type of charts, are the candlestick charts. Although the necessary information is the same as the bar chart, they are widely used because of their ease in quickly determining the information.

Candlestick charts are preferred by some because the view is easier to see the color variations indicating up and down days.

See Figure 3-5 below:

The narrow wick of each candle is the day's trading range. The fatter portion, the body on the candle, is the area between the opening price and the closing price. Open candles are positive, meaning the stock closed at the top of the open body. This is the same as the bar chart showing the 'Tick' on the right side of the bar as the closing price. The darker candles are negative, meaning the stock closed at the bottom of the body. In other words, it opened higher for that day and fell to close at a lower price.

Let's look at the difference in bar charts and candlestick charts. Candlestick charting gives precisely the same information as the bar chart as you can see in the following picture; the candlestick is more colorful and more natural to assess the information quickly.

The following is a comparison of Candlestick vs. Bar Chart.

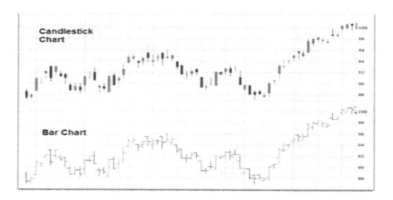

Candlesticks Defined

What does the Candlestick look like?

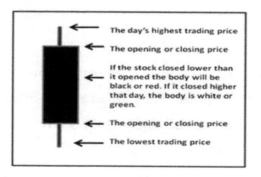

What does Red (or Black) Candlestick Mean?

The color of the candlestick tells us whether that candle was formed by a positive trading day (advance in price) or a negative day (decline in price). If the closing price is lower than the day's opening price, then the body of the candle is red or black. See the following picture:

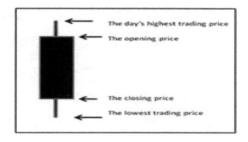

Note: Most charting software allows you to customize your charts to reveal your desired colors. This enables you to choose your personal preference as to the color for your OPEN candles and for the CLOSED candles.

How about the White Candlestick?

The white candle, also known as the "OPEN" Candlestick, shows the price move up.

The bottom of the white body represents the opening price and the top of the body represents the closing price.

Thus, this candle will represent a positive "CLOSE."

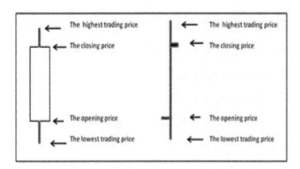

In the other comparison, you can see that the Bar and Candlestick charts would say the same thing. They simply look different.

Let's look at some very familiar 'indicators.' Candlesticks form based solely on the price movement and many of the candles are very telling. They are great indicators of what is likely to happen soon concerning the price of the stock. Many of these candles have been given names to identify them. So let's look at each one and learn the importance it has when seen on a chart.

DOJI

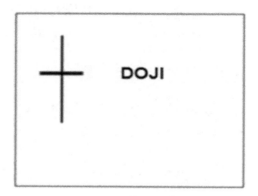

DOJI is a name for candlesticks that form when a stock's opening price and closing price are virtually equal. This DOJI tells us that during the trading day, the stock moved higher and lower and neither the buyers nor sellers were more prominent. It says the stock traded up and the sellers stepped in and traded lower and the buyers stepped in. When just looking at a DOJI it appears very uneventful. Still, when combined with other candles and trends, it can be very telling.

When thinking in the perspective of a market trend moving higher or a downward trend moving lower, the DOJI is a very telling sign that the number of buyers and sellers has become equal. Therefore, after the market or stock has been in a trend, either up or down, and suddenly a DOJI is formed, then this tells us that since the buying and selling has equaled out — then a reversal of the current trend may be ahead.

The Shooting Star

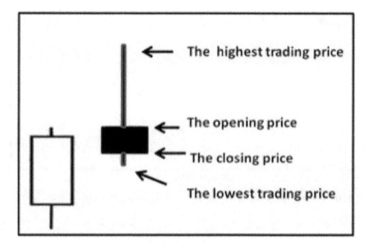

The Shooting Star is a Bearish candle that forms after an advance in the stock or index price. Try to think of it in this manner. The price has advanced for several candles, or days, and tries to continue the advance. It opens and trades higher, creating the tall wick on top of the candle, but then the sellers take over, forcing the price back down to close near the opening price. This is an early indication that the advance has lost its momentum. Technically, according to the above picture, the closing price would need to be below the opening price. However, that is not always the case. Meaning, if you simply switched the open and closing prices on the above picture, it would still indicate an early warning for a reversal, maybe just not as pronounced as the close that is lower than the open. But it would still be a warning sign.

The Evening Star

By itself, the DOJI at the top of the formation would just be a DOJI, meaning the opening and closing prices were virtually equal. But when the dark candle forms the following day indicating a change in direction, then this DOJI becomes what is called an Evening Star.

The large white candle preceding the DOJI indicates buyers jumping in after a significant advance. The Evening Star indicates inability to move higher, and the Bearish Engulfing candle the following day confirms the sellers have entered the market.

Another very important Candle is called the Hammer.

The Hammer

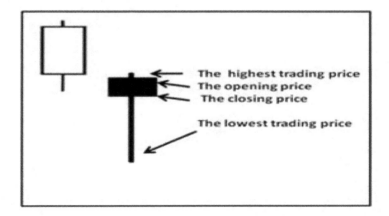

The Hammer is normally found at the bottom and forms when a stock has been in a downtrend and finally reached a support level. It is very similar to a mirror image of the Shooting Star at the top of an advance.

When this Candle forms at the top of a pattern after an advance, it is called the Hanging Man. Both look very similar and can have either a positive or negative body.

Some prefer one, some prefer the other. The two charts say the same thing – they just simply look different. So use whichever one you prefer.

CHAPTER 3:

Futures Trading

Ｔhe most important thing a futures trader learns is that the buyer never actually takes possession of the commodity. Professional investors who have traded in pork bellies would not know what a pork belly looked like if a truckload was dumped in their driveway. You don't need to invest in a refrigerating plant to trade frozen concentrate orange juice, and you don't have to acquire grazing land to invest in cattle futures.

What is being traded back and forth is a contract that specifies a date sometime in the future when the holder of the contract is required to deliver a quantity of the commodity for a predetermined price. In that futures contract, everything about the transaction is spelled out — the quantity and quality of the commodity, the exact price per unit, the date it is expected, and how it will be delivered. These are real-life transactions, and there are real sellers and real buyers and real products involved. Still, unless there is a mistake, you will not be the last one holding the contract and responsible for its execution.

The Futures Contract

A futures contract is a legal agreement at that, to buy or sell a specific instrument at a preset price at a specific time in the future.   The futures contract's underlying asset could be stocks, commodities, currencies, bonds, and other instruments. The terms of a futures contract are standardized in quantity and the delivery date. The exchanges facilitate trading between buyers and sellers. To trade futures, traders need to put up cash, commonly referred to as margin in futures trading. A proper margin must be maintained for the life of the trade.

Margin

Traders need to have sufficient margin to trade futures. This will usually depend on the kind of future that is being traded and how many contracts. To fully understand the margin, there are three different types of margin to understand.

Initial Margin

The initial margin is the amount that is required to execute a futures trade. This amount is typically set and facilitated by them. The real exposure of the trade can be greater than the initial margin. If the loss of trade becomes greater than the initial margin, it may prompt a broker's margin call. If a broker issues a margin call, traders are expected to post margin to bring the account back up. Futures accounts "marked to market" daily by brokers. This means that futures contracts are re-evaluated at the end of each trading day. The profit and loss are added and subtracted from the margin daily.

Example of Initial Margin

The exchanges set initial margin for futures, and this amount usually varies from 5%-15% of the contract. This can also vary from broker to broker. Let's use the following example.

A trader wants to get into a wheat contract for $50,000, and the initial margin percentage is set to 10% for wheat futures contracts.

The initial margin amount the trader would need to post is only $5,000. The important thing to note about the initial margin is that it can be subject to change by the exchanges if volatility picks up.

Clearing Margin

Clearing Margin is money that is required for brokerages and institutional firms to have on hand to complete futures transactions with their clients. It is a form of capital protection for brokers to have to ensure client trades are executed.

Maintenance Margin

The maintenance margin is the minimum amount of cash a trader must maintain in their account to keep a trade open for a futures contract. If the net value of the account falls below the maintenance margin, this will prompt the broker to issue a margin call. Once a margin call is issued, the trader must post more funds to bring the account value above to the minimum.

Settlement in Futures

When a trader enters into a futures position, he or she has three different options as to how they can settle the trade.

Straight Cash Settlement

This is most common when a certain future doesn't have an option for physical delivery.

Physical Delivery

In today's day, physical delivery is very uncommon. Less than 1% of futures contracts take physical delivery of the underlying asset. If it does happen, the contract's amount specified is delivered by the seller of the contract to the actual exchange. It can happen with commodities, but it's very rare.

Let's say, for example, you had one contract on wheat futures. The standard contract size for wheat futures is 5000 bushels. When the contract expires, you can take physical delivery of 5000 bushels of wheat. Even though most brokers will only do cash settlements, it is worth noting that there is a very small percentage that takes physical delivery. I don't know about you, but I prefer cash over wheat any day.

Expiration

The futures contract's expiration date is when that futures contract stops trading and gets the final settlement price for that specific period. Most brokers typically expire a trader's position by closing their trade out and giving them the option to re-open it for the new contract month and at the new contract price.

Regular Closeout

This is the most common closeout. A trader closes out their futures position at the current market price. Many day traders use a regular closeout and typically don't hold long-term positions until expiry for futures.

Different Types of Futures Contracts & Codes

A futures contract can technically be created on anything. All you need is two different counterparties to create the transaction. They don't necessarily have to happen through the facilitation of exchange. It is best to trade futures that are facilitated and standardized by an official exchange. Since futures are a standardized contract, they have specific symbol structure and abbreviations. Futures contracts can be traded on the following markets.

- Agricultural
- Currencies
- Equity Index
- Financial
- Meats/Dairy
- Metals
- Softs

It is important to note some of the futures codes and abbreviations that you might see on your trading platform. Below are the abbreviations for each contract month.

- F= January
- G= February
- H = March
- J= April
- K=May
- M=June
- N=July
- Q= August
- U=September
- V= October
- Z= December

Getting familiar with how contracts work is important before beginning to trade them. It is also very important to remember when certain futures contracts expire before actually beginning to trade them. Futures contracts are a very risky trading instrument but can be the fastest and most liquid instrument to trade. Futures contracts tend to have great liquidity, low spreads, and predictable volatility.

CHAPTER 4:

Which Market to Trade in and
Which Broker to Use

I f you are brand new to trading, you are probably curious about how you would sell or purchase security. Any time that the market is open, there are going to be two prices for any security that can be traded. There will be a bid price and the asking price. The bid price is what buying or purchasing traders are offering to pay for that stock right then. The asking price, on the other hand, is the price that traders want to sell that security.

You will quickly notice that the bid price is always going to be a bit lower simply because the buyers want to pay less. The asking price is still going to be higher because sellers want more for their holdings. The difference between these two prices is known as the spread.

The spreads that are found will vary for each stock, and they can even change throughout the day. If a stock doesn't have a ton of buyers and sellers, then there could be a more significant spread. When there are more buyers and sellers, then the spread between these two prices will be much lower.

As a swing trader, when you are ready to enter into a position, you are going to have two choices. You can either go in or pay the price that the seller is asking for right away or you can place a bid that is at or below the bid price. Paying the asking price immediately can be beneficial because it ensures that the purchase transaction is completed or filled but may mean that you will pay more for it. When a trader places a bit at or below the current bid price, they may be able to purchase at a lower price. But there is the risk that no seller will want to sell for the lower price, and the order may not get filled.

Then, you can enter into the trade and complete the rest of your strategy.

Investment and Margin Accounts

There are two types of accounts that you can choose to open to trade stocks. The two main options include the margin account and the investment account. With a margin account, you can borrow against the capital that you have placed in your account. The investment account, on the other hand, will allow you to buy up to the dollar value you hold in that account. You are not able to spend more than what you have put in that account at a time.

When you decide to open up a margin account, you may be able to borrow money from the investment or brokerage firm to help pay for some of your investment. This is a process that is known as buying on margin. This can provide you with some advantages of purchasing more shares that you would be able to afford if you just used the capital in your account, and it can help you leverage to get more profits with your money.

However, there is a catch with this one in the form of more risks. When you borrow the money to make your investments, there will come the point when you must pay the loan back. If you earn the profits that you think you will, it is easy to pay this back. But, if you lose out and make the wrong predictions, you are going to have to find other ways to pay the money back. Making investments with leverage can magnify the percentage losses on your money.

As a beginner, you should stick with a regular investment account. Trading on margin can increase the amount of risk that you are taking on in your trades. This may be tempting because it can increase your potential profits, but there is a lot more risk that comes with it as well. You will do much better going with an investment account instead. This way, you can pull out the money that you are comfortable with rather than hoping that you make a right prediction in the beginning when you are learning.

Picking out a Broker

If you have already gotten into other forms of trading in the past, then you can work with the same broker that you already have. But, if you are getting into trading and this is the first one you have done before, then you will need to search to find the right broker for you.

There are many different brokers out there, and many of them can assist you with swing trading. The biggest thing that you will want to look at is the commissions and fees that each broker assesses against you. Since swing trading times are relatively short and you will enter into and out of trades within a few weeks at most with each trade, you want to make sure that the profits you make aren't eaten up by the commissions to your broker.

There are different methods that the broker can use to come up with their fees. Some will charge a fixed rate for the whole year. This often works well for long-term trades and probably won't be an option available to you since you will make more trades. The two options that you will most likely deal with include a fee for each trade or a fee based on how much profit you earn.

Find a broker who will earn a fee based on your profits. This way, you are not charged a ton if you make a bunch of trades during that time. If you earn a good profit, you will have to pay a bit more because of the percentage. If you receive less on one of your trades, then you won't have to pay the broker as much as you did before.

Before you enter into any trade, make sure that you discuss the fees with your broker. They should be able to outline their payments and can discuss with you where your money will go when you work with them. This can help you to get a good idea of how much you will spend based on how much you earn, how many trades you decide to enter into, and more. Get the commissions and fees in writing, along with any other agreements that you and the broker and their firm agree to protect you.

Picking out How Much You Want to Invest

Since we have already know the importance of working with an investment account rather than trying to do the trading on margin, you will need to decide how much money you would like to put into your account.

First, talk with your brokerage firm and decide how much you need to put in to meet their requirements. Some brokerage firms will ask you to spend a certain amount or keep a certain amount in your accounts at all times in order to trade. If your chosen firm has that kind of requirement, then make sure that you put in at least that much. Putting in more is up to your discretion.

If there isn't a requirement for a minimum, it is best to start out by putting in an amount that you are comfortable losing. No one hopes to lose money on any of their trades. But it does happen, especially when you are a beginner. Putting in just the amount that you would be willing to lose if something goes wrong can help to reduce the amount of risk that you are taking on.

Getting started with swing trading can be exciting. This is a fun type of trading that moves quickly and can help you to earn a good profit in a short amount of time but still doesn't require you to spend all day on the computer watching how the trade is going. By following some of the tips above, you will be all prepared to take on some of your first trades with this strategy.

CHAPTER 5:

Utilizing Binary Options

C urrently, binary options are trendy among investors working on the Internet. There are a lot of rumors and other extremely conflicting information about them. Thus, binary options for novice traders, on the one hand, offer excellent prospects; on the other hand, they pose a danger.

Beginner traders should remember three universal truths:

- binary options can become the basis of your financial well-being;

- easy money is just an element of advertising from brokerage companies;

- success is achieved only by those investors who are willing to work hard for months and years.

Essence of Binary Options

We are talking about a simple financial instrument that anyone can use, even without special skills and knowledge in exchange trading. Its essence is to make a forecast on the direction of the movement of the value of the selected investment asset.

In other words, the trader must choose to increase or decrease the price of, say, the currency Euro/American dollar (EUR/USD) after a predetermined period called the expiration period of the binary option. If the forecast is accurate, then the investor will earn 70–80% of the transaction amount. If it turns out to be incorrect, then the entire amount delivered will be lost.

It should be understood that when trading binary options with one of the many brokerage companies, the assets themselves are not acquired. That is, the money of the trader, regardless of the amount of the transaction, does not leave the broker's website. However, this does not stop making money on the investment instrument in question.

A beginner should trade binary options using the minimum possible rates of 1 dollar. Do not rush to play big. First of all, you should acquire the necessary experience and trading skills.

Also, you need to be aware that in this industry, the earnings of successful professional traders and the brokers themselves are provided by the lost investments of loser investors. In order not to become a representative of the latter, it is necessary to work hard and hard.

- **Do not believe in a freebie**

All binary options brokers attract new customers with incredibly easy money. However, the reality is much less optimistic. The number of loser traders will always significantly exceed the people who have achieved success in this field. Otherwise, such financial activities will cease to be profitable to their creators.

To obtain a stable profit, the trading system used by the trader must have an efficiency of at least 60–65%. Otherwise, it will get difficult for you to cover the loss from unsuccessful transactions.

Also, it should be understood that most of the trading indicators and strategies laid out in the public domain, without your refinement and twist, will not be able to provide a trader with a stable income.

If you want to get guaranteed high results, you will have to understand:

- reasons and directions in the movement of financial markets;

- the impact of news on stock trading;

- the basics and methods of conducting technical analysis;

- selection and personalization of trading indicators.

Only by independently following the described path from beginning to end, can an investor succeed.

Popularity of Binary Trading

Nothing is surprising in the popularity of binary options among novice traders. The whole secret lies in their incredible simplicity. Indeed, the entire task is that the investor should just guess the movement of the price of the asset. Also, brokerage companies tactfully hold back that many take years to learn this.

Also, an alternative to binary options is real trading on currency, stock, or commodity exchange. This area of investment is not an example of more complex. To work on transactions, a trader has to deal with a vast array of information and learn hundreds of particular terms. For instance, you need to deal with pips, take profits, and stop loss, and so on.

Principle of Binary Options

First of all, the trader needs to choose one of the investment assets available from the broker used. This can be a currency pair, company stocks, indices, or commodities. This is done in 2 clicks.

Then you need to decide on the direction in which the quotes of the underlying asset will move and set the expiration date (time for which the transaction is concluded).

Now you need to press one of the two keys: Call or Put. A call should be chosen if the investment asset has risen in price after a specified period. On the contrary, Put is responsible for lower quotes.

After the start of the binary option, we are waiting for its execution. For example, if the expiration period was 5 minutes or M5, then after this time, we either earn a successful forecast or lose the money delivered.

Bulls and Bears as a Trend Direction

The trend on the stock exchange is the direction in which the asset price moves at a particular time interval. It is easy to guess that quotes can go down, go up, or standstill. The latter scenario is infrequent and can occur only in the shortest segments.

When the price of an asset rises, it is customary to call this trend upward or bullish. The bulls with their horns, as it were, throw its value up.

It is incredibly crucial for any binary trader to be able to determine what the succeeding trend will be. Indeed, in this case, he is guaranteed to make a profit. True, for a beginner, this task will be challenging for some time.

When it is More Profitable to Trade

Binary options transactions are concluded for the movement of the price of exchange-traded assets. Naturally, trading is focused on the operating time of the largest world exchanges. If desired, the trader can trade around the clock for five business days. At the same time, there are certain time intervals at which you can achieve better results.

The most auspicious periods are:

- from 11.00 to 12.00;

- from 16.00 to 19.00;

- from 3.00 to 9.00.

All intervals are given in Moscow time. There is no secret in these segments. They represent the time of intersection in the work of various major exchanges: European, American, and Asian.

Besides, you need to understand that a particular day of the week also affects the success of binary options trading. The best trading days for professional investors are Tuesday and Wednesday.

How to Choose an Expiration Period

Currently, most binary options are for one minute to half an hour. There is an interesting pattern: the less experience a trader has, the less a short expiration period he prefers.

Indeed, it seems to beginners that the optimal duration of a binary option is 60 seconds. This position has a clear rationale. Indeed, using such an expiration period in work, one can conclude much more transactions during the day than when working on longer time intervals. It is.

The problem is different. The shorter the expiration time a trader works, the more serious the investment risk. In fact, at 60-second intervals, price movement is complicated to analyze and predict. Consequently, the percentage of successful transactions is reduced.

It is generally accepted that informed and high-precision trading is carried out with expiration dates M15 and M30. That is, at 15- and 30-minute intervals.

Do not confuse expiration with a timeframe

The concept of a timeframe refers directly to the settings of the trading chart. This is the name of the period that will be described by one Japanese candle or bar.

There is a general rule that beginners should be guided by. The timeframe should equal the expiration date. In other words, if you make a deal for 5 minutes, then in the chart settings, you should choose the same timeframe.

Trading Chart

For the convenience of trading, the underlying asset quotes are usually traced within the framework of trading charts. This method is the most intuitive and convenient. Each of the binary options brokers on the market offers its customers its version of such a map. However, their problem is that these electronic trading floors have an extremely meager set of indicators for technical analysis.

To solve this problem, most professional traders resort to the following trick. They get used to working on at least two windows. The first displays the site of their brokerage company, where they only enter into transactions. The second displays a full-fledged live schedule.

A legitimate question arises — where to get it? We recommend our readers to get their version of free trading for the Meta Trader 4 exchange trading. It has in its arsenal a live schedule that fully meets all the highest requirements.

Besides, you can use the services of several free online services:

- Trading View;

- Free Stock Charts;

- Think or Swim;

- Ninja Trader.

Charm of Japanese Candles

Japanese candles are usually called a variation of the most popular type of chart for trading binary options. In addition to it, there are also linear and bar. However, they are less convenient and much less commonly used by traders.

So, each Japanese candlestick demonstrates the direction of movement of the asset value in each time interval or timeframe. If the minute timeframe is selected, then every Japanese candle on the trading chart will display the price behavior for 60 seconds.

Candles in 2 colors are presented on any chart. Some display an upward price movement, while others show a downward motion. As a rule, bullish candles are green and bearish red. However, some binary options brokers do not observe this point. There is nothing to worry about because the specific choice of colors does not affect anything.

CHAPTER 6:

How to Evaluate and Compare Stocks and Other Securities

Mutual Funds

Shared funds pool several investors' properties, supplying purchasing power that surpasses that of all but the wealthiest individuals.

Suppose you have $10,000 to invest. If you try to spread out the cash Around 50 stocks, commission costs alone may cripple you. Yet spend the same $10,000 in a mutual fund that holds 50 stocks and you've got that. Buy a small piece of each of those companies without the cost or trouble of acquiring them separately.

Professional money managers decide when the fund sells and buys, and all of the financiers either win or lose together. If shared, the investment pays 10% in one year, and every person who holds the fund at the beginning of that year will see the fund—very same 10% return on his investment.

At the end of 2012, financiers worldwide had $26.8 trillion purchased Mutual funds, with $13.0 trillion of these assets in the hands of the U.S. cash supervisors, according to the Investment Company Institute

(ICI). Of that, $13 trillion bought the U.S. shared funds, 45% remained in stock funds, and 26% were in bond funds.

Stock and bond mutual funds can be found in two tastes:

Passively handled funds

Frequently called index funds, quietly managed funds try to match the performance of an index.

Actively handled funds

Unlike passively managed funds a proactively handled funds purchase and offer securities to exceed the return of their standard. Generally, index or index party. It's hard to overstate the value of mutual funds as a financial investment automobile. More than 92 million people own in the United States alone shared funds, frequently through retirement plans. Additionally, most 401 (k) retirement plans invest employees' possessions in pooled funds, so if you take part in a company-sponsored retirement plan, you probably currently own funds.

Pros:

- **Professional management**

The majority of individuals do not know much about evaluating financial investments because of a lack of interest, absence of training, or both options.

With almost 9,000 standard mutual funds on the market, practically any investor can find a fund to resolve her investment objectives.

- **Diversification**

Portfolios containing a range of stocks or bonds tend to be less unpredictable than an individual stock or bond. Mutual-fund supervisors utilize their purchasing power to acquire numerous securities, which, most of the time, supply diversity.

Cons:

Every shared fund charges fees. Remember that specialist you worked with when you purchased the mutual fund? Some funds also charge costs called loads, gathering additional money to compensate for the salesperson or investment company.

- **Complacency**

Mutual-fund investors typically presume that considering that they have a professional handling a diversified basket of stocks, they can relax and relax. Don't make that error.

- **Poor returns**

Many academic studies recommend this pattern isn't brand-new, which fund fees should have much of the blame. While the persistent underperformance shouldn't scare you away from shared funds, it needs to hammer home the significance of choosing your money wisely.

Exchange-Traded Funds

According to the ICI, by the end of 2012, creditors had invested around $1.34 trillion in exchange-traded funds commonly called ETFs. ETF possessions correspond to barely more than 10% of the value of standard shared funds, but these types of financial investments continue to grow in appeal. ETF possessions have more than tripled considering in 2006, while the number of ETFs on the market increased to 1,239 in 2012, from 359 at the end of 2006.

ETFs operate much like mutual funds because they blend the resources of many financiers to acquire a basket of stocks, bonds, or both. ETFs vary from traditional shared funds in a couple of important ways:

Switch on platforms

As the name suggests, these securities are traded on almost the same markets as stocks. ETF rates change from second to second, just like stock prices.

Mostly index funds

While a couple of ETF managers actively handle their funds in an attempt to top standards, the bulk of them tracks indexes.

Greater openness

Unlike traditional mutual funds-- which the SEC requires to divulge their holdings quarterly-- ETFs need to disclose daily. Considering that indexes don't change their holdings typically, a lot of ETFs don't either.

Pros:

- **Convenient trading**

Unlike the way shared funds, reprice at the end of the day and trade only at that cost during the following day, ETF costs rise and fall intraday like stocks.

- **Hedging**

Financiers can purchase and sell options on ETFs, just as they can on the majority of Inventory. Starting buyers will probably avoid stocks, but the flexibility to buy and make choices. ETFs permit has contributed to their popularity.

- **Trading costs**

Numerous brokers charge more to trade mutual funds than stocks. When investors buy or offer exchange-traded shared funds, they pay the same commissions charged for stock trades.

Cons:

- **Fund costs**

Bear in mind that every shared fund charges fees. Since ETFs trade like stocks, investors often treat them like stocks and forget about those charges. And ETFs rarely draw much attention to the fees they gather.

- **Selection**

Many ETFs track indexes, indicating they're passively managed. While some ETFs use active managers, financiers looking for active management will discover a couple of choices amongst ETFs.

- **Viewed complexity**

While ETFs appear like mutual funds in the majority of aspects, many investors avoid them. A 2010 survey by Mintel Compere Media, a consulting firm, found that almost 60 percent of financiers decided not to buy ETFs because they did not understand how they operated.

Certificates of Deposit

Standard Deposit Certificates (CDs) serve as enhanced savings accounts. Investors lend money to a bank that then consents to pay a fixed interest rate — usually for a term of 5 years or less.

Whereas creditors can withdraw cash from a savings account at any time, CDs need to keep the bank's funds until the date of maturity. These tend to pay higher interest than traditional cost-savings plans because of this limitation.

CDs can't change any of the other financial investments pointed out. They supply you with a way to produce more interest on your money holdings than you'd obtain from a bank cost savings account or a brokerage account.

Pros:

- **Security**

Like other bank accounts, CDs are guaranteed for up to $250,000 by the Federal Deposit Insurance Corporation (FDIC) in the event the bank stops working. Brokerage accounts do not receive FDIC protection, though the Securities Investor Protection Corporation (SIPC) does provide similar, if less extensive, defense.

- **No fluctuation**

Since your funds remain in cash, they won't decrease in worth.

- **Simplicity**

If you understand cost savings accounts, you already understand much about how the CDs running.

Cons:

- **Low is returning**

Although CDs usually deliver more interest than bank savings accounts, they will pull all the other investment groups mentioned over the long term.

- **No liquidity**

CDs tie up your money for some time. You can access the cash if you need it, but you'll pay an early withdrawal penalty or forfeit some of the interest.

- **Separate accounts**

Many investors buy stocks, bonds, and shared funds from institutions other than banks. If you keep your money in a bank CD, you must keep it at the bank, which indicates you can't redeploy it to buy stocks or bonds up until you move the money to a brokerage account.

Alternative Assets

When you dip your toe into the market, you may hear about different investment options, including the following:

Nearly 100 commodities trade on markets worldwide. Financiers can gain commodity exposure by acquiring stock in a business that deals with those products, or they can invest straight via a futures contract. Futures contracts allow investors to purchase or offer products and other assets for predetermined rates in the future.

These derivatives enable stock or ETF financiers to bet on whether shares will rise or fall without purchasing Shares themselves. Suppose the stock trades are worth $50 per share. If the stock is $55, you can either buy the stock at a discount rate or sell the call option at a profit.

Hedge funds

These entities pool financier money like shared funds do, but they tend to pursue unusual or esoteric methods. Hedge funds, gently managed and often deceptive, frequently handle massive threats.

Precious metals

Investors purchase valuable metals as a hedge against inflation, or as a backstop to safeguard wealth versus a disaster, assuming that when catastrophe wrecks the monetary markets, metals such as gold will retain their value.

Antiques

While financiers can generate income in antiques, many lack the marketplace competence to profit regularly.

Of course, plenty of financiers value the inflation protection and total-return potential of real estate and would like to purchase. Since some estate cost so much, a couple of people have funds to invest straight in the property beyond their houses. These companies purchase, offer, and handle real estate, and their trust units' trade on exchanges like stocks.

Weighing the Options

No matter how completely you examine the choices for prospective investment, how much caution you take in crunching the numbers, how much time you take to research the stock exchange, and the forces that impact it, you're going to make errors. A great deal of them.

Extreme boasting about returns and success rates is among the best methods a newbie can find the posers. Boasters end up being especially aggressive during bull markets-- when lots of stocks are hitting brand-new highs. If you're listening to the wrong voice, you're going to end up high, dry, and perhaps ashamed when the market corrects.

Before you buy into some pundit's sure-fire strategy, do some of your work.

Stocks

Common stocks supply financiers with an ownership interest in a company. Shares of stock represent business equity and are called equities. Financiers can purchase and offer stocks on exchanges entities that exist mainly to produce a market for the shares. Stocks trade continuously during business hours: 9:30 a.m. to 4.00 p.m. Eastern time most weekdays with prices changing from 2nd to second.

As the value of business fluctuates, so does the cost of an investor's stock. Over the long haul, stock rates tend to rise when companies increase their earnings and sales. However, in the short-term, stocks can gyrate moved by things like total financial patterns, news from rival companies, government action, and other aspects.

At the end of August 2013, Microsoft shares sold for $33.40, with about 8.44 billion shares outstanding. If you increase the number of shares by the per-share cost, you get $282 billion, the stock's market capitalization, frequently abbreviated to market cap. A financier acquires 50 shares of Microsoft for approximately $1,670 would own a small portion of one of the world's largest companies. When more people wish to purchase a particular stock than to offer it, prices tend to increase. As any economics book will tell you, when items end up being scarce and the demand for them increases, prices often increase in reaction.

CHAPTER 7:

Technical Analysis

Technical analysis is basically a strategy that is going to be used to help us evaluate investments and identify some of the different forms of trading opportunities by looking at all of the statistical trends that have been gathered up over time with the trading activity. The trends that are sometimes studied here are going to include volume and price movement.

Unlike what we are often going to see when we work with a fundamental analysis, this kind of analysis is going to look at a lot of charts and graphs in order to find the patterns of price movements, look at some of the trading signals that are out there, and even look at some of the other analytical charting tools to figure out the weakness or the strengths of a security.

There are a lot of ways that we are able to work with a technical analysis based on what our needs are at the time. It means this strategy works on currencies, fixed income, commodities, stocks, and futures, to name a few. For our needs, we are going to look mostly at how it works with stocks, but there are a lot of options out there that we can explore and find good opportunities for investing with this technical analysis.

This one is going to assume that the security is already priced right where it should be. With fundamental analysis, the investor believes that they can find a security that is discounted based on its perceived worth, lack of debts, equity, assets, and more. But technical analysis is going to assume that all of this is found in the price of your security already and that there is no such thing as an overpriced or discounted security at all.

There are going to be two main methods that are going to be used to analyze securities and make some good investment decisions, and these are the technical analysis and fundamental analysis. Fundamental analysis is going to involve us going through some of the financial statements of a company to help determine the fair value of the business.

To keep it simple, the technical analysis is going to spend a lot of time trying to look more at the sentiment of the market behind the trends in the price by looking for trends and patterns and seeing how that may affect what is going on in the market. This is preferable to a lot of investors, especially with a day trader, rather than looking at some of the fundamental attributes that may be found with the security.

How to Use a Technical Analysis

This is a strategy that is going to spend a good deal of time trying to forecast some of the price movements of pretty much any instrument that you would want to trade, as long as it is going to be, on the average, subject to the different forces of supply and demand. This means that you are able to work with a technical analysis of currency pairs, futures, bonds, and stocks.

In fact, there are some who view this kind of strategy as just a study of the supply and demand forces and that these are going to be shown as the price movements of the market on some of the graphs and charts that are used. You will find that this kind of analysis is going to most likely, apply to some of the price changes, but there are a few analysts of this nature who will track numbers in addition to the price, including the open interest figures and the trading volume.

Across the industry, there are going to be lots of signals and patterns that are developed by researchers in order to help us see the benefit of working with this kind of analysis and getting the best results I the process. These analysts have also come in and developed many systems of trading to help them forecast what is going to happen in the market and trade on those price movements.

Some indicators that we will want to use are more focused on figuring out the trend in the current market, including the resistance and the support areas, and then there are some that are more focused on determining the strength of a new trend and how likely it is that this trend is going to continue along the way. Some of the technical indicators and charting patterns that we are able to use will include momentum indicators, moving averages, channels, and trendlines.

Technical analysts have also developed a lot of trading systems in order to make it easier to forecast and then trade on a price movement.

To keep this simple, a technical analysis is going to look at the following indicators to help make things possible, including:

1. The support and resistance levels
2. Moving averages
3. Oscillators
4. Volume and momentum indicators
5. Chart patterns
6. Price trends

The Limitations of a Technical Analysis

While there are a lot of different parts that come with technical analysis, there are also a few limitations that we are going to notice when it comes to working with technical analysis. The major hurdle that is going to come in is the legitimacy of the economic principle of the efficient market hypothesis. According to this, the market prices are going to reflect all of the past and current information already, so there is no way for us to take advantage of the patterns or the wrong prices in order to earn some more in profits.

Many fundamental analysts and economists are going to believe that inefficient markets will find that it is hard to believe that any actionable information is contained in the historical price and volume data, and furthermore, that history is not going to repeat them. Instead, they believe that prices are going to move more as something that is random.

Because of this, you are then going to see some of the other traders look at the price decrease and choose to sell their positions to avoid losing money. This is going to reinforce the trend as well.

Even with some of these shortcomings, there are a lot of benefits to working with the technical analysis. There are a lot of traders, especially those who are working with day trading, who will work with this method because it is going to provide them with the results they need. And knowing the movements of the charts will often be enough to help them to see success with this kind of trading since it is shorter in length. But doing a combination of the fundamental analysis and the technical analysis has served a lot of traders in the process as well, so it depends on your trading style and what seems to work the best for you.

CHAPTER 8:

Understanding Futures

Futures are a derivative form of financial contracts that oblige the related parties to perform a transaction with an asset at a future price and date that has predetermined. In futures trading, the buyer required buying, or the seller needed to sell the underlying securities at the price that has set, no matter what is the current price in the market or what the expiry date. The underlying assets comprise of physical commodities and other instruments of financing. They are standardized as well for facilitating trading on a futures exchange. You can use futures for speculation of trade or hedging.

- Stock futures, for example, the S&P Index
- Commodity futures, for example, natural gas, crude oil, wheat, and corn
- U.S. Treasury futures related to bonds and various other products
- Precious metal futures for silver and gold
- Currency futures including pound and euro

Pros of Futures Trading

- The investors can use up contracts of futures for speculating right on the direction in the set price of the underlying assets.

- Companies have the chance of hedging the raw material price or the products sold by them for protecting themselves from adverse movements of the cost.

- The contracts of futures need a deposit of only a portion of the amount of contract with the broker.

Cons of Futures Trading

- Investors have the risk of losing more than the starting margin amount as futures use up leverage.

- Investing in contracts of futures might lead a company that hedged to miss the favorable movements of the price.

- The related margins might act as a double-edged sword. The gains will amplify, and so will be the losses.

Instead, the broker will need an initial amount of margin, which includes a part of the total cost of the contract. The amount that will be held by a broker can differ relying on the contract size, the terms and conditions of the broker, and the investor's creditworthiness.

Speculation of Futures

The speculators will also be able to take a sell speculative or short position if they think that the price of the underlying security will be falling. If the asset price declines, the trader will be taking an offset place for closing the futures contract. Once again, the difference will get settled at the expiry date of the futures contract. An investor can make a profit when the price of the underlying asset is below the cost of the contract and will incur a loss of the present rate is more than the price of the contract.

It is essential to note that margin trading will permit a more significant position than the actual amount held by the account of the brokerage. As the final result, investing on margin can improve the percentage of profits but can also maximize the losses. For example, when a trader has a brokerage account balance of $5,000, and he is in a trade for a position of $50,000 in crude oil. If the oil price moves in the opposite direction of the trade, the trader will incur a loss that can even exceed the $5,000 margin amount of the account. In such a case, the broker will be making a margin call for additional funds that need to deposit for covering the losses of the market.

Futures Hedging

Futures can use up for hedging the movement of the price of the underlying security. The primary goal here is to prevent losses from the inherent nature of unfavorable changes in price rather than speculating. Most of the companies that opt for hedges are producing or using the underlying security. For instance, a farmer of corn can start using futures to lock in a particular selling price for their crop. By doing this, he can potentially cut down the risk and also guarantee that he can receive a fixed amount of pay. If by chance, the corn price falls, the company will be gaining on the hedges for offsetting the losses from selling the crop in the market. With such a form of loss and gain offsetting one another, hedging can effectively lock in a high price in the market.

Futures Regulation

The markets of futures regulate by the CFTC or Commodity Futures Trading Commission. CFTC is a form of a federal agency that was set up by Congress in the year 1974 to ensure integrity in the market price of futures. It also included the prevention of abusive practices related to trading, regulation of the brokerage firms that are related to futures trading, and prevention of fraud.

Example of Futures Trading

Suppose a trader is willing to speculate on the crude oil price by entering a position in the contract of futures in May. He enters the position with the expectation that the crude oil price will go up by the end of the year. The crude oil futures of December traded at $50, and the trader fixes in the contract at that price. As crude oil is traded in the increment of 1,000 barrels, the trader is now holding a position that is worth $50,000 in crude oil ($50 x 1,000 = $50,000). But, the trader is only required to pay out a part of the total amount upfront, the initial amount margin that is needed to deposit with the related broker.

In the period between May to December, the crude oil price will fluctuate exactly as the futures contract price. In case the price of crude oil turns out to be too volatile, the broker might ask out for extra funds that need to deposit into the account of margin. In December, the expiry date of the futures contract is approaching, which is the third Friday of that month. The overall price of crude oil rose to $65. Now, the trader sells out the original futures cOntracts for exiting his position. The total difference will be cash-settled. They will earn a total of $15,000, excluding the commissions and fees of the broker ($65 - $50 =$15, $15 x 1,000 = $15,000).

But, if the price of crude oil came down to $40 in place of rising up to $65, the trader will be losing $10,000 ($50 - $40 =$10, $10 x 1,000 = $10,000).

Futures are an excellent form of investment when appropriately used. It would help if you determined the market conditions accurately for gaining profits.

CHAPTER 9:

Fundamental Analysis and Technical Analysis

I f you want to succeed as a trader, analyst, or investor, then you have to learn and understand fundamental analysis. It constitutes one of the most crucial aspects of any investment or trading strategy. Many would claim that a trader is not really accomplished if they do not perform fundamental analysis.

Fundamental analysis can be defined as the examination, investigation, and research into the underlying factors that closely affect the financial health, success, and wellbeing of companies, industries, and the general economy.

It can also be defined as a technique used by traders and investors to make a determination regarding the value of a stock or any other financial instrument by examining the factors that directly and indirectly affect a company's or industry's current and future business, financial, economic prospects.

At its most generic form, fundamental analysis endeavors to predict and learn the intrinsic value of securities such as stocks. An in-depth examination and analysis of certain financial, economic, quantitative, and qualitative factors will help in providing the solution.

Fundamental analysis is mostly performed on a company so a trader can determine whether or not to deal in its stocks. However, it can also be performed on the general economy and on particular industries such as the motor industry, energy sector, and so on.

Basics of fundamental analysis

The main purpose of fundamental analysis is to receive a forecast and thereby profit from future price movements. There are certain questions that fundamental analysis seeks to answer. For instance, an analyst or swing trader may wish to know answers to the following questions;

- Is the firm's revenue growing?

- Is it profitable in both the short and long terms?

- Can if afford to settle its liabilities?

- Can it outsmart its competitors?

- Is the company's outlook genuine or fraudulent?

These are just a few examples of the numerous questions that fundamental analysis seeks to answer. Sometimes traders also want answers to questions not mentioned above. In short, therefore, the purpose is to obtain and profit from expected price movements in the short-to-near-term future.

Most of the fundamental analysis is conducted at the company level because traders and investors are mostly interested in information that will enable them to make a decision at the markets.

They want information that will guide them in selecting the most suitable stocks to trade at the markets. As such, traders and investors searching for stocks to trade will resort to examining the competition, a company's business concept, its management, and financial data.

For a proper forecast regarding future stock prices, a trader is required to take into consideration a company's analysis, industry analysis, and even the overall economic outlook. This way, a trader will be able to determine the latest stock price as well as predicted future stock price. When the outcome of fundamental analysis is not equal to the current market price, then it means that the stock is overpriced or perhaps even undervalued.

Steps to Fundamental Evaluation

There is basically no clear-cut pathway or method of conducting fundamental analysis. However, we can break down the entire process so that you know exactly where to begin. The most preferred approach is the top-down approach. We begin by examining the general economy followed by industry group before finally ending with the company in question. In some instances, though, the bottom-up approach is also used.

Companies are often compared with others. For instance, we may want to compare energy companies Exxon Mobil and British

Petroleum. However, we cannot compare companies in different industries. For instance, we cannot compare a financial company like City Group with a technology firm like Google.

Determine the Stock or Security

You need first to have a stock or security in mind. There are many factors that determine the stocks to trade. For instance, you may want to target blue-chip companies noted for exemplary stock market performance, profitability, and stability. You also want to focus on companies that constitute one of the major indices such as the Dow Jones Industrial Average or S&P 500. The stocks should have large trading volumes for purposes of liquidity.

Economic Forecast

The overall performance of the economy basically affects all companies. Therefore, when the economy fares well, then it follows that most companies will succeed. This is because the economy is like a tide, while the various companies are vessels directed by the tide.

There is a general correlation between the performance of companies and their stocks and the performance of the general economy. The economy can also be narrowed to focus on specific sectors. For instance, we have the energy sector, transport sector, manufacturing, hospitality, and so on. Narrowing down to specific sectors is crucial for proper analysis.

There are certain factors that we need to consider when looking at the general economy. We have the market size, growth rate, and so on.

Basically, when stocks move in the markets, they tend to move as a group. This is because when a sector does well, then most companies in that sector will also excel.

Company Analysis

One of the most crucial steps in fundamental analysis is company analysis. At this stage, you will come up with a compiled shortlist of companies. Different companies have varying capabilities and resources. The aim in our case is to find companies that can develop and keep a competitive advantage over its competitors and others in the same market. Some of the factors that are looked into at this stage include sound financial records, a solid management team, and a credible business plan.

When it comes to companies, the best approach is to check out a company's qualitative aspects followed by quantitative before checking out its financial outlook. We shall begin with the qualitative aspect of the company analysis. One of the most crucial is the company's business model.

Business Model

One of the most crucial questions that analysts and all others ask about a company is exactly what it does. This is a simple yet fundamental question. A company's business model is simply what the company does to make money. The best way to learn about a company's business model is to visit its website and learn more about what it does. You can also check out its 10-K filings to find out more.

You need to make sure that you thoroughly understand the business model of each and every company that you invest in. Most companies have very simple business models. Take McDonald's for instance.

They sell hamburgers and fries. At other times it is not easy to understand what a company does. For instance, the world's best-known investor, Warren Buffet, does not invest in tech companies because he simply doesn't understand what they do.

Stock Analysis

Stock analysis can be defined as the process used by traders and investors to acquire in-depth information about a stock or company. The analysis is done by evaluating and studying current and past data about the stock or even company. This way, traders and investors are able to gain a significant edge in the market as they will be in a position to make well-informed decisions.

Technical Analysis versus Fundamental Analysis

When analyzing a stock, analysts usually perform both fundamental and technical analysis. Fundamental analysis relies mostly on different sources of data such as economic reports, financial records, market share, and company assets. For publicly listed companies, the data is usually sourced from financial statements such as cash flow statements, income statements, footnotes, and balance sheets.

Such information is readily available to the public via 10-K and 10-Q reports. You can access the reports via the EDGAR database system that is managed by the SEC or Securities and Exchange Commission.

Data can also be sourced from companies' earnings reports which are often released quarterly.

Intrigues of Fundamental Analysis

Some of the parameters that analysts look at within a company's financial statement include a measure of solvency, profitability, liquidity, growth trajectory, efficiency, and leverage. Analysts also use rations to work out the financial health of companies. Examples of such ratios include quick ratio and current ratio. These rations are useful in determining a company's ability to repay short-term liabilities based on their current assets.

To find the current ratio, you will divide the current assets with the current liabilities. These figures can easily be accessed from the company's balance sheet. While there is no ratio that is considered ideal, anything below 1 is considered a poor financial situation that is incapable of meeting all short-term debts.

The balance sheet also provides analysts with additional information such as current debt amounts owed by the company. In such a situation, the analysis will focus on the debt ratio. This is computed by working out all the liabilities and dividing by the total assets. When the ratio is computed, a ratio greater than 1 point to a company with a lot more debt compared to its assets. This means that should interest rates rise, then the firm may default on its debts.

This will give a trader or investor a feel of the company's performance and will determine whether the firm is stable, receding, or growing.

It is also common for an analyst to compare a company's financial statement with those of other companies in the same sector. This is done in order to compare profitability and other parameters.

Of great importance is the operating profit. It is a measure of the revenue that a company is left with after other expenses have been cleared. Basically, a firm with operating margins of 0.27 is viewed favorably when compared with one whose margin is 0.027, for instance. This can be translated to mean that the firm whose operating margin is 0.27 spends 73 cents per dollar earned to foot its operating costs.

Financial Statements

Fundamental analysis at the company level would be incomplete with analyzing the company's financial performance. There is often more than one financial document available. In fact, most companies produce or generate numerous financial statements that it becomes difficult to understand them all. Most often, they present investors with a huge challenge. However, with a little bit of information and exposure, you can understand these financial documents. This is advisable

Technical Analysis

The fact is that fundamental analysis is such a broad subject that what it entails sometimes differs depending on scope and strategy. It involves a lot of things such as regulatory filings, financial statements, valuation techniques, and so on.

83

CHAPTER 10:

Techniques and Tactics

The thing to keep in mind is that the best strategy of a day trader is to find something that works and repeat it over and over again.

Once you have decided on that one strategy that works for you, placing and entry, setting a stop loss, and making a profit, then get on the simulator and practice! That's the way you will work out issues with your strategy. You can go over it as much as you want until you see a continuous profit.

The goal is to be able to control your risk. You want to be able to manage your trade risk and your daily risk.

- The amount you are willing to risk on each trade is referred to as your trade risk. That should ideally be equal to one percent or less of your capital on each trade. You can do that by selecting an entry point and then set yourself a stop loss. The stop loss will get you out of the trade if the odds go too much against you. You should also learn how to calculate the position size for futures, stocks, and forex because knowing your position size will also help to keep your risk low.

- The amount that you lose in a day is your daily loss. It is smart to set a daily loss limit each day to avoid huge losses to yourself. If you have set your trade loss at one percent, you may want to set your daily risk at three percent. In that instance, you would need to lose three or more trades with zero winners to lose three percent. And if you have practiced using your software and practiced using your strategy, that shouldn't happen often. You want to keep your daily losses small so that on winning days, they are easily recouped.

Trading only two or three hours per day is very common for day traders. However, some make a trade for the whole session from nine-thirty am until four pm, usually for the US stock market. All-day traders are consistent in the hours they trade. They trade at the same hours each day, whether they are trading for three hours or the whole session. Here are some of the hours you will want to focus on yourself:

- If you are going to be trading stocks, the best time of day for trading is the first hour and second hour right after the open, and the last hour of the day before the close. So, between 9:30 am, and 11:30 am EST is the first two-hour period you want to find good trades. The biggest price moves and biggest profits are to be at this time of day. Between 3:00 pm and 4:00 pm EST is a good hour of the day also. There are pretty big moves then also, however, if you are going to only trade for two hours in a day, then trade in the morning. That's when the market is the most volatile.

- If you will be trading futures, the opening time is the better time to trade. That would be between 8:30 am, and 11:00 am EST. Active futures see activity around the clock, so the best trading times are a little earlier then with stocks. Futures markets officially close at different times, and the last hour of a contract can also offer sizable moves for you to get in on.

- If you decide to trade the forex market, they trade twenty-four hours a day during the week. The EURUSD is the favorite of the day traders. It is the most volatile between 0600 and 1700 GMT. These are the hours when the day traders should trade this market. The biggest price moves are between 1200 and 1500 GMT. This is when both the US and London markets are open, trading the euro and US dollar.

We mentioned before that day, traders find a strategy and then repeat it over and over again. That is what we will talk about now in more detail. These are the basic day trading strategies that are used. There are many others, but these are the most common.

Scalping: Probably, the most common of the strategies is scalping. It is a primary get in there and gets out of there type of mind frame toward trading. Day traders will get in on a good trade and then sell as soon as it starts to show profitability. It's relatively safe, and that's why a lot of people like it. You don't watch it and then hope it stays strong.

Daily Pivots: A day trader using this strategy would look to buy their trade at its lowest price during the day and then try to sell it at its highest price of the day. These times are also referred to as low of the day (LOD) and high of the day (HOD).

Fading: This is known as a risky strategy. Day traders will short stocks once they start to gain rapidly. The theory being that the stocks are over purchased, and the traders who purchased early will be looking to sell because the stock is gaining and they are making money. The other traders may be scalping. This strategy of fading can be profitable when used correctly, but keep in mind that the risk is higher.

Momentum: If you are a person who would be interested in riding trends, then this type of trading may be a perfect strategy for you. The day traders who enjoy this method watch the current news and are watching for the trends being supported by the highest volumes of trades. Then they jump on the wagon and ride the waves until they see signs of it turning around. Then, of course, they are watching the news releases, and they just start all over again.

Stop Losses: The use of stop losses is crucial in day trading. The market is so prone to sharp price movements, and you could potentially see substantial losses in a short amount of time if you aren't careful. There are two types of stop losses which we covered earlier: the physical stop-loss order and the mental stop loss. During your whole day trading career, it is essential for you to keep these stop losses in the front of your mind.

These strategies that I have given you are not miracle strategies. Just because you master one, it won't make you rich. The main secret lies in consistency. Always be looking at your strategies and evaluating them. Tweak them to work for you by adding other parts of other plans to them. Use them to find your comfort zone. Find what works for you. It has taken many of the most elite day traders' years to hone and perfect their unique strategies.

If you are to be a successful day trader, you must have patience. You may wait minutes to days for a profitable trade to come along. You must be able to make smart decisions. Knowing when to get in and out of a trade is vital. There could be a profitable situation staring you in the face, and you have maybe minutes to react. And of course, you must be able to maintain balance. How you respond to winning and losing is so important. One day, you can be on cloud nine because the day went perfectly. The next day you could be down in the dumps and depressed because you may have taken a nasty loss. You must maintain balance there for your emotional wellbeing.

CHAPTER 11:

Stock Market

T he stock market has a long history, dating back hundreds of years. The first company to ever go "public" and issue paper shares of stock to investors was the Dutch East India Company in Europe in 1602. This company also was the first to issue dividends, with yields that went as high as 62% annually.

Traders received paper notes when they purchased stock, which they bought and sold with other traders throughout Europe. Soon the London Stock Exchange was born in England, and then the New York Stock Exchange (NYSE) in the United States (both of which are still operating today). Like the NYSE, exchanges provided a centralized location for companies to go "public," as well as for traders to buy and sell shares of these companies' stocks. Considering many citizens lived miles away from these stock exchanges, and the automobile wasn't invented yet, "bucket shops" started propping up throughout the United States.

You could compare a bucket shop to Vegas sports betting, as the shops would allow traders to place wagers on the direction of stocks, without actually owning any shares. These bucket shops were entirely speculative and risky, in that traders could get up to $100 worth of stock buying power with a deposit of just $1. This ultimately meant traders could lose a lot of money "betting" on stocks. Soon bucket shops were made illegal, as they were thought to be the cause of two market crashes in the early 1900s.

But even in the era of bucket shops, exchanges have always acted as the centralized hub for stocks, and stock records, to be kept. As such, these exchanges needed to maintain a permanent record of the price of public companies. Instead of computers, stock prices were listed on "ticker tape" at these early exchanges, mostly stock symbols and prices being communicated via telephone lines, and printed out on long strips of paper via a typewriter. You may hear traders say phrases like "read the tape," which is a reference to the ticker tapes used many years ago.

By the mid-1960s, ticker tapes were replaced with electronic "ticker boards." These were long electronic displays where ticker symbols and prices scrolled across a screen. These "ticker boards" were soon shown at the bottom of television screens on news channels. Traders would have to sit in front of their TV and wait for their stock symbol to scroll across the bottom to know the real-time price.

Up until the 1990s, most people could only trade stocks via "stockbrokers." Traders had to call their "broker," who would then buy or sell stocks for them. Most of these brokers worked on a fixed commission, meaning they charged a fee to traders to use their services. It was costly to trade stocks back then, with commissions being as high as $100+ for just one order.

With the internet boom of the '90s, online retail brokers started emerging who offered commission fees around $20 per trade. With the huge savings offered to consumers, many jumped in, even those who may not have qualified before due to small account sizes.

As the years have gone by, brokers have slowly been in a race to the bottom in regards to commissions, lowering their fees to $10, then $5, then $2.50, and now almost all have switched to commission-free trading. The beauty of capitalism allowed for increased competition and made the market a much less expensive place for us as stock traders. Many brokers also now offer no account minimums, meaning someone with as little as $100 can open an account and trade stock, all with no fees.

This all equates to our current era being an excellent time to be a trader and invest in the stock market. This is because no matter your job or net worth, you can grow your wealth in the markets and not be burdened with the large fees which accompanied stocks in the past.

What's a Stock?

At its most basic, one share of stock represents a partial claim to a given company's earnings and assets. The more shares of a company's stock available, the less each share is worth. The more shares of a company you own; the more control you have over the company. Stock can be referred to as equity or shares as well. Those who own stock in a company are referred to like that company's shareholders which means they each get a share of profits, known as dividends, at predetermined periods throughout the year and also, in some cases, voting rights based on the number of shares in a company that they hold.

While originally, each stock that you owned came with a physical piece of paper indicating what you owned as well as how much, these days all of this information is stored electronically by the brokerage that you will ultimately choose to handle your transactions directly. While holding a physical copy of your shares is nice, it would also require you to take those documents to the brokerage you were using every time you wanted to trade. This process is referred to as the in-street name method of holding shares.

While owning shares of a company does entitle you to a piece of their profits, it does not mean that you can have an active say in how the business is run, even if you own voting shares. At most, you will be able to vote for the board of director members at an annual shareholders' meeting. During this meeting, you will be able to cast your vote, and it will be weighted based on the number of shares of the company's stock that you hold. This process aims to provide shareholders a way of indicating their pleasure or displeasure with the overall way the company is being run. Unless you own a significant portion of the total number of shares of a company, you really won't have much say in what they do.

Types of Stocks

There are ordinary shares, which are the most widespread, and we have spoken so far preference shares and savings shares. The preference shares give the right to a preference in the distribution of profits or the repayment of capital. Savings shares do not have the right to vote but have patrimonial privileges established by the company's deed of incorporation. If you have bought an action, you also have the right to receive an annual dividend—that is, the company profit divided among all the participants in the so-called "risk capital." High dividends are very attractive to investors, but it is not guaranteed that they are distributed every year or even that they are constant for budgetary reasons or for company policies that do not provide for profit distribution to favor the company's capitalization.

According to some variables, the market value of a share is that which results from the official price lists, if listed, and may be different from the nominal value and the asset value (net equity divided by the number of shares). A solid company with good growth prospects will be associated with high potential and, therefore, a high value of the shares issued; on the other hand, a company with financial problems and with prospects of de-growth will be associated with a low value of its shares. Even the performance of the economy, politics, and speculation can influence an action's market value.

Stocks as Investment

In general, it is possible to invest in the stock market with the direct purchase of listed shares or with the purchase of derivatives. In general, for those who have the problem of how to start investing in the stock exchange, the recommended choice is that of derivatives, in particular, binary options. For those who want to buy the securities directly, the process is slightly more complex—you have to open an account for the custody of shares, and on this deposit, you, unfortunately, pay a salty stamp.

Another way to invest in the stock exchange is made up of mutual funds. Investments of this type do work through the purchase of a share of the fund. The managers then use the money obtained through the sale of shares to invest in the stock exchanges. This is an indirect investment that delegates all responsibilities to fund managers. In some cases, good profits can be made, but it has often happened that investment funds, especially if managed by Italian companies, have led to very strong losses. Moreover, the tax treatment of this type of investment is strongly penalizing.

Mindset and the right approach

The right investment attitude, essentially, is a blend of six key characteristics. Over time, it is the right contributing approach that will have the impact between an acceptable auditor and a dependably productive financial expert.

Mental balance is the key

What do we fathom by mental prudence? It is the ability to think indisputably despite when markets are unusual, and the financial expert is under tremendous weight. Usually, this is when the most financial expert will as a rule sway and accept veritable contributing failures. Believe it or not, mental aptitude is about the calm that you can keep up despite when the market appears to go against you. There are two extreme perspectives on mental balance. Stock exchanges are driven by fear and insatiability. Financial experts will find ordinarily when all is said in done, get energetic at the most elevated purpose of the market, and terrible at the base of the market. Smart contributing is connected to doing the cautious reverse.

Not just peace of mind; you also require balance

How is balance unique in connection to peace of mind? What makes a difference is extremely unnoticeable, however, notwithstanding all that it exists.

Do whatever it takes not to seek after returns, seek after the right framework

If you are more focused on the results rather than the technique, if you are more worried over the closures than about the strategies, by then, you have an attitude problem to contributing. Remember, contributing is substantially more of getting the framework right. How you recognize stocks, how you screen stocks, what are the non-cash related parameters you consider, how might you impact on the channel and the boundaries of security, how might you incorporate a motivation by aligning your passage and leave levels; all these are a bit of your methodology or system. Your consideration should be on fulfilling this methodology, and the results will thusly come after.

The act generally determined and be a self-motivated student

The stock exchange is a remarkable teacher yet to take in the fundamental activities from the market. You should be an excited observer and a self-motivated student. The best way to deal with gain from the market is to listen energetically to what the market is trying to tell you. Endeavor to record the learnings from the market consistently and it can transform into your Bible for exchanging.

An ounce of movement justifies a pound of orchestrating

You can make the best of plans within the planning stage before trading. There are a couple of things about the stock exchanges that you can adjust just once you start exchanging with real money.

CHAPTER 12

Cryptocurrencies

To be able to get a better understanding of what cryptocurrency is, it is important to not only define it but also go beyond the definition to cover its technical and financial aspects.

Definition of Cryptocurrency

We do not have a universal definition of cryptocurrency. However, for purposes of our discussion, we can define cryptocurrency as:

Cryptocurrency is a virtual decentralized digital currency created and managed through advanced algorithmic encryption techniques known as cryptography.

Features of Cryptocurrency

Cryptocurrency has many features. However, we can classify these features into three main categories: technical features, financial features, and transactional features.

Technical features

- **Virtual** – This currency has no physical existence. It is generated by using electronic codes

- **Algorithmic** – Codes generated are algorithmic by nature

- **Cryptic** – The codes are encrypted as a guarantee of security. They also regulate the creation of new coins and verification of existing coins.

- **Database-driven** – Code records are stored in database ledger known as the blockchain.

- **Decentralized** – Most fiat currencies are created, supplied, and controlled by governments' central banks. On the contrary, cryptocurrencies creation and transactions are algorithmically self-controlled by open-source software. They rely on peer-to-peer networks for their circulation. Thus, no single entity can control its creation and circulation.

- **Digital** – Traditional fiat currency is defined by a physical object such as gold, silver, etc. They are also stored in vaults. Digital currencies are not defined by any physical object, but codes. They are kept in digital wallets which act as their store. They are transacted by transmitting them from the sender's digital wallet to the recipient's digital wallet.

- **Adaptive scaling** – While traditional fiat currencies are controlled through monetary authorities' interventions, cryptocurrencies can scale up or down dynamically (automatically) to control their supply in the market.

- **Mining** – While traditional coins are produced through a process of minting, crypto coins are produced through a process of mining.

- **Open source** – The software used to create mine cryptocurrency has codes that can be readable by any software developer. Thus, developers can create their APIs without the need to consult or seek permission from anyone.

- **Proof-of-Work** – Most cryptocurrencies (Bitcoin included) rely on the proof-of-work system. In this system, a hard-to-compute but easy-to-verify puzzle is used as a way of earning the fundamental value of the coin. Thus, a token (coin) is created once a puzzle forming it is cracked (solved). Some other cryptocurrencies use Proof-of-Stake or Proof-of-State either as a substitute or in addition to proof-of-work.

Financial features

- **No physical jurisdiction** – The currency is not limited to a given territory. It is global and universal.

- **No legal jurisdiction** – Because it has no physical jurisdiction, it is not subject to laws of any country.

- **Electronically transacted** – The currency is transacted in electronic form.

- **A measure of value** – The currency is used to measure value based on 'proof of work' (PoW), and other measures.

- **Exchange of value** – The currency can be used as a reward for the exchange of goods and services.

- **Speculative** – The currency is market-driven and, as such, is subject to the forces of demand and supply.

- **Controlled supply** – Most cryptocurrencies have an upper limit of supply tokens. For example, Bitcoin has a maximum of 21 million tokens that are expected to be completely mined by 2140. This supply is controlled by a schedule written in the code. This shows transparency in terms of the money supply so that anyone can know the number of tokens in circulation and roughly compute the number of tokens available by a given future date. This is unlike fiat currency, whose volume in circulation is mostly kept secret by governments around the world.

- **No debt** – Cryptocurrencies are currency commodities just as gold. They stand for themselves. Unlike fiat currency, they do not represent debts (through the system of IOU).

- **Value** – For a currency to have worth, it must represent some value. Before the advent of fiat currency, traditional currencies used to represent actual gold. Gold is scarce and hard to mine and refine. Therefore, the work undertaken in this process of mining and refining contributed to its fundamental value. Furthermore, its scarcity granted it the market value (the forces of supply and demand). Mining crypto coins, especially Bitcoins, requires a lot of work and increasingly complex and sophisticated circuitry. This makes Bitcoins scarce.

Transactional features

- **Secure** – While public keys are transmitted with the coin transaction, only the owner of a cryptocurrency has the private key. Thus, this is the only one who can send cryptocurrency. This sophisticated cryptography is made harder to break by the sheer magnitude of the big numbers that represent it.

- **Pseudonymous** – Cryptocurrencies use pseudonyms such that neither transactions nor accounts are connected to the real-world identities. For example, Bitcoins are sent and received via randomly generated addresses. Each of these addresses is around 30 characters. Coin-holder identification is encrypted within this address. While you can use these randomly-generated addresses to follow up on transaction flow, you cannot connect to users' real-world identity with those addresses. While the accounts are pseudonymous, they are not anonymous as they are publicly available. However, some cryptocurrencies like Monero have both pseudonymous and anonymous features.

- **Permission-less** – There is no permission-seeking arrangement when it comes to using cryptocurrency. Cryptocurrencies are generated by software that anyone can easily download for free and use. Once you have downloaded the software, you can easily send cryptocurrencies such as Bitcoins. There is no one to prevent you from doing so.

- **Irreversible** – After a transaction is confirmed, it can never be reversed.

- **Quickly available around the globe** – Cryptocurrency transactions happen almost instantaneously. Within a few minutes, networks around the globe confirm them. Distance does not matter.

How Do Cryptocurrencies Work?

Cryptocurrencies work on the same concept as debit cards. The only difference is that bookkeeping is not done by banks but by the public. They have no centralized clearinghouse. Their bookkeeping is jointly carried out through blockchain — a publicly available and distributed ledger across networks.

Since every person has a copy of the ledger/register, transparency, and accountability help to build trust. By not being distributed, it avoids intermediaries who would be responsible for the storage of the register. With no intermediaries, no agency costs.

The following concepts make it easier to understand cryptocurrency:

- Mining
- Public Ledger
- Transactions

Mining of Cryptocurrency

Mining is a special term that refers to the process of validating the algorithm of a given token. It is only when a given token is validated (verified and confirmed as genuine) that it becomes a cryptocurrency and thus is entered into the public register (blockchain).

Those people who carry out this mining are the ones referred to as miners. Miners' role is to secure the network by receiving and validating new issues of coins and entering them into the public register. This verification process involves using software to solve cryptographic puzzles of a given set of transactions and adding them to the ledger once they are solved. Miners are rewarded in the form of coins for their mining effort.

For heavily mined cryptocurrency such as Bitcoin, miners require specialized and sophisticated hardware such as aspic chips to process billions of calculations per second to confirm one transaction. The more puzzles miners solve; the more cryptocurrencies they earn. This incentivizes them to continue mining, thus ensuring the safety of transactions over the network. This mining process gives fundamental value to the coins. This is what is referred to as proof-of-work.

Blockchain Technology

A blockchain is a public ledger of cryptocurrency transactions. When a peer-to-peer transaction is made, the transaction is transmitted to all network users with 'full-node' wallets. Miners then try to solve the transaction's cryptographic puzzle. The first miner to solve the puzzle is rewarded with a few newly mined coins. Every transaction belongs to a block with a cryptic link to another block. Therefore, when a transaction is solved, its cryptic link to the new block is unraveled, and the new block is added to the ledger. This cryptic link serves as a chain between the previous block to which the transaction belongs and the new block unveiled through the cryptic link. This is why it is called a blockchain. Nonetheless, before the ledger is updated, there has to be a consensus among miners as to its validity. This consensus is proof that the miner who was the first to solve the cryptic puzzle has done work (proof-of-work).

In a technical sense, cryptocurrencies are restricted entries in a database of which certain specific conditions must be met for there to be a change in these entries. Assuring that these conditions have been met is achieved through proof-of-work. Thus, a mathematical algorithm rather than people secures the entries, unlike in the traditional fiat currency system.

Transactions

A transaction is a transfer of funds between two digital wallets. This transaction is transmitted to a public ledger. Once transmitted, it is queued awaiting verification and confirmation by miners. The wallet originating a transaction encrypts it with a cryptographic signature (encrypted electronic signature) as a mathematical (algorithmic) proof that the transaction is originating from the owner of that particular wallet. Once miners verify and confirm the validity of the cryptographic signature, it is then that they enter it into the public register (ledger/blockchain).

The cryptographic signature has a public code, which matches up with the user's privately held password. Any user of a given cryptocurrency can choose to have access to the ledger by downloading it. This becomes a "full node" wallet. However, they can opt to keep their coins in a third-party wallet such as Coin base.

Whoever owns the private key (private password) to a given a wallet owns the amount of cryptocurrency denoted in the ledger (blockchain). The primary difference between banknotes and cryptocurrency is that instead of governments and banks issuing the currency and keeping ledgers, an algorithm does.

How Do You Acquire a Cryptocurrency?

There are two ways to acquire cryptocurrencies:

- Purchase them
- Mine them (validate their algorithm)

How cryptocurrency avoids double-spending

Double spending is a situation whereby a person uses the same currency unit to spend more than once. Digital products are much easier to duplicate than non-digital products. However, due to the cryptic and accounting nature of cryptocurrency, it is nearly impossible to carry out double trading. Cryptocurrency uses blockchain technology to avoid any likelihood of double-spending.

Why do you need a cryptocurrency?

The following are the main reasons why people go for cryptocurrency:

- **Safe hedge** – What has propelled Bitcoin is its storage of value. Bitcoin has become the virtual gold standard for virtual currency. This is because, like most cryptocurrencies, their volume is known in advance.

- **Speedy transaction** – Due to their digital nature, cryptocurrencies enable fast transaction processing.
- **Low-cost transaction** – Cryptocurrencies use the peer-to-peer transaction process. Thus, middle agents, such as banks and clearinghouses are eliminated.
- **Anonymity** – Cryptocurrencies allow the anonymous transaction process.

CHAPTER 13:

Portfolio Rebalancing and Management

Most investors have their portfolios arranged by class in percentages. They may want to seek out a certain level of aggressive growth, a certain level of value investing, and they also might want to protect a certain amount of their capital. In other words, they use asset allocation to build a portfolio that helps the investor to meet his or her goals over the long term. Asset allocation refers to the way that you have distributed your investments, so for example, if we were talking about asset allocation over stocks and bonds, an investor might have 50% of their investments in stocks and 50% in bonds, while a more aggressive investor looking for more growth with higher risk tolerance might have 70% of their investments in stocks and 30% in bonds.

When you first build your investment plans, determining your asset allocation is going to be one of the first things that you do. Someone who needs to raise cash quickly is going to be devoting more of their investments to aggressive growth stocks. Someone who is looking to preserve their money is going to be putting more of it into bonds or money market funds. Everyone has different goals, and you will have to look at your own goals and then breakdown your investment allocations accordingly.

Once you have that setup, you are going to let your investments run for a year and be making your stock purchases at regular intervals in order to meet your goals. So if at the beginning of the year you've decided to invest 65% in stocks, 20% in corporate bonds and 15% in cash, at each point when you make investments you will divide them up this way.

Of course, some investments are going to over perform, and others are going to underperform, with time. So by the end of the year, your portfolio might not be structured in the way you set out to have it structured. You might find that instead, you end up with 70% in stocks, 25% in corporate bonds, and 5% in cash.

At the end of the year, it's time to look at your asset allocation and see if it's remained the same. You will also have to look at your own goals. At the end of the year, your goals might be different than they were at the beginning of the year.

In any case, what you're going to have to do is rebalance your portfolio, either to stay consistent with your original goals or to change the portfolio so that it will help you to meet your new goals. If the percentages in each asset class have changed, and you want to stay consistent with your original goals, you may have to buy and sell assets in order to bring things back into alignment.

Using the prior example, we would have to sell off some stocks and corporate bonds in order to reduce their percentages in the overall portfolio. Then, you would reinvest the proceeds as appropriate to bring yourself back to 65-20-15.

Diversification

The most important tactic that you can incorporate into your investing is diversification. The reason is pretty simple and straightforward. First of all, no matter how careful you are in your fundamental analysis, mistakes are going to be made. Also, companies are not always going to stay on the same track going forward. A company might be on solid footing now, but the management may make many mistakes in the coming years, or there could be changes in management or competitors can arise that outcompete the company that you thought was a great investment, causing it to falter.

We have no control over these things. Therefore, the best method that can be used to protect you is to avoid putting all of your investment money in a single company. In fact, you should avoid putting all of your investment money into a small number of companies. The more companies that you invest in the better off you are, at least in theory.

In practice, you should select a set of companies that you can comfortably manage. The specific number of companies is going to vary from person to person. The more companies that you pick, the more time you are going to have to devote to fundamental analysis and keeping track of stocks and company earnings reports going forward. So there are going to be limits which are different for each person and their living situation. Someone who is a fulltime investor may be able to keep track of a few dozen companies. But someone who has a "day job" and isn't available for more than a few hours a week as far as devoting time to their investments, is not going to be able to keep track of more than a handful of companies.

Therefore, we can't say what the exact number of companies to invest in should be. That is going to depend on your situation, but we can say that one company is certainly a bad idea, and 3-4 companies are certainly not enough. Most financial advisors would agree that at a minimum, you should be investing in 7-10 companies. Many financial advisors believe that a good number to shoot for is 20 companies.

Diversification helps to protect you against these types of risk factors. At a minimum, invest in three different sectors or industries. Then invest in three different companies per sector.

Dollar-Cost Averaging

The tactic that is used by long term investors is called dollar-cost averaging. The purpose of this method is to avoid getting in a situation where you are buying too much of your stocks when prices are high. As you know, stock prices are constantly fluctuating up and down, and the market itself has many highs and lows, including bull and bear markets that take pricing of individual securities along with it for the ride.

Now, over the long term the truth is no matter what you do, the odds are that in ten, twenty, or thirty years, prices are going to be much higher than they are today and so the individual fluctuations are not going to matter that much. But as an investor, you want to maximize your return on investment or ROI. In order for that to happen, so that you can grow your wealth to the maximum extent possible, you need to be buying at the best possible times, when you can get the best possible prices.

And that is none of us has a crystal ball despite the claims of some to the contrary. It's simply impossible to know at any given moment whether or not the price of a stock is the best price that is going to be available.

During a bear market, many people are interested in being able to buy stocks when they are "cheap" relative to what they are normally priced. This is a good goal to have, and during bear markets, one of the things that you might consider doing is accelerating your stock purchases.

Any time that you have extra money to invest, you can do this outside of your regular dollar-cost averaging investment plan. Remember that the rules should be followed but they are not something that has to be written in stone, and adjustments can be made when they are warranted.

Buy More during Downturns

Any time there is a stock downturn, whether it's an individual stock or the market as a whole, you should immediately buy more stock. This is one of the reasons that it's important to have cash on hand. Of course, you don't want to use up all of your cash on a single stock purchase. If it does keep dropping in price, you are going to want to be able to buy more stock at the lower prices. But whenever there is a downward trend in price, you want to put money into the markets so that you can buy the stock at a discount. Of course, we are talking about normal circumstances here. If there is bad news about a company coming out, such as the company is engaged in some kind of fraudulent activity that is probably not a good reason to be investing more in the company.

By mundane we mean one bad earnings report among an overall trend of increasing profits. Investors that unload all their Apple stock based on one quarterly report that misses "expectations" or even shows reduced profits are making a foolish play.

External causes can be economic or political in nature. These are news events and such that lead to overall market declines that turn out to be temporary. In fact, these are the reasons that you should use in order to buy more shares.

CHAPTER 14:

Disciplined Approaches to Investing

Whenatrader gets into trading, they are very hopeful that everything will play out well and that in no time, they will start making a lot of profits. To succeed in trading, it is essential that a trader know what trade is all about. This means that they should fully be aware of the strategies in trading, risks involved, and how to manage the risks, and also importantly, understand the psychology involved in the trade.

Understand Your Motive

It is essential to understand what you are about to put yourself through. Understand why you want to venture into trading, is it because you want to make money or because others are doing it? Knowing your primary motive for joining trading will save you from losing money. Trading involves you invest your money into the investment. Therefore, before you invest your money, it's good to learn all that trading entails. Without understanding the market, you are likely to lose money in ways you would have avoided had you first taken some lessons. Trading sounds so easy to someone who has not gotten into it, but along the way, they find out that it was not as easy as it seemed. Therefore, for a beginner trader, it is essential that they fully understand the business before investing in large sums of money. It is vital that as a trader, you understand how to stick to your methods no matter how tempting it gets. Sticking to your strategy shows that you trust your understanding of the market and cannot easily quit.

Never Stop Learning

For a trader, there's never enough knowledge of the market. The trading patterns keep changing; you need to keep learning why the changes are taking place. You also need to know what to do with the changes and what strategies will work. Learning the basics and understanding the trading market is essential, but a trader has to be more open to learning every time. For a successful trader long-term trader, they have to keep up with new technologies that may affect the market. This means keeping up with the world's happenings as that is what will affect the trade market.

Realize Your Goal

Understand your trading goals, as this will help you push on when the market doesn't seem to be working out well for you. The primary purpose of trading is to get money, but you should have a reason for why you need the money. Having the exact reason in your mind why you need the money will keep you more motivated to be a better trader every day. A clear objective will make you want to keep going even when you feel like giving up.

Identify Your Flaws as Well as Your Strengths

Immediately you start trading. It is essential that you identify your weaknesses. The earlier you learn about your shortcomings, the quicker you get to work on it before you are exposed to losing money. You will get to know if the weaknesses are something you could work on by yourself, or you will need help from other experienced traders. It is good, however, to try working by yourself first since then, that means that you get to learn your weaknesses further. When this doesn't work out, then it is good to seek help from other traders. Identifying your strength is essential as it will help you stop wasting time when you can follow your strengths to achieve an intended trade goal. This will also help you schedule your time well so that you are able to balance your weaknesses and strengths. Every trader is different; what one trader finds to be their weakness could be another trader's strength and vice versa. The trick is to identify what will do for you as a trader. The trader, therefore, has to find out where they are going wrong and amend or replace the mistakes for better trading experiences.

Allow Yourself Time

Traders get into the market with so many expectations about the market. They imagine that they will enter the market, put some money and the next minute they are swimming in millions of moneys. Trading is profitable when done right, but it also needs time before you finally enjoy your benefits. Allow yourself time to adapt to the market, to know how trading actually works, and even understand the many risks you are likely to incur. Allowing yourself time to just adjust to the market without so much greed for the money will make you a very great trader who will succeed in the long run. It is better to make small profits for a long time than to make huge profits for a short while. Not being ready is essential for a trader; it will give him the patience to wait and work towards being great traders rather than just focusing on being short term traders. It will also make the trader love their trading experiences because they are not rushing themselves or putting too much unnecessary pressure on themselves.

Have a Network of Fellow Traders

Like all other businesses, traders are supposed to create friendships among themselves. These fellow traders will not only inspire a trader, but they will offer help to the trader when the trader needs it. It is good to have friends doing the same thing as you are as you get to hear their experiences, and you can compare them with your own experiences. Having friends who been in trading longer than you have will give awareness of what awaits you in the long run. You can get some things to copy from a friend who has been doing this ahead of you. Having friends who are in the same industry will also give you a friend counselor or mentor who will help you in making various trade decisions. You can make this advisor your mentor whom you will consult from time to time. A mentor will help you avoid making bad trading decisions that could cost you a lot of money and also help you identify how to work out your weaknesses. A network is generally crucial because even other than having people who will offer you help;

you also have people who can give you future connections in the market.

Love the Trading Market

To love the trading experience means that you enjoy the process more than your love for the money that comes along. By doing this, it means that even when you don't get so much money from the process, you will push on with the trade because you love the thrill of trading. The benefits are vital without them; there would be no reason to do trading. However, the benefits will not be very rewarding for someone who does not enjoy the process of getting them. This is even more so because you may lose all the money you had invested in trading, but if you love the process, you will know how to pick yourself back up. The rewards are not very fulfilling for a trader if the trader does not enjoy his journey and keeps waking up to make the trade just for the money. Enjoying the process gives you reasons to take more risks that will yield you more profits. But when you do not enjoy the process, you only play safely to maintain the same earnings as you make every day. If you are able to maintain a standard point, you do not really care for anything else. Loving the process means that you get to explore more to understand the market and also to find ways that will make you enjoy your work more. When you love trading, you are not like to be as exhausted when working as people who do not enjoy it. When you enjoy the trading process, you are likely to adjust to the market quickly and even succeed more than traders who have been doing it for long.

Stick to What You Know

The trading market is diverse; stick to what you are comfortable in rather than wasting your time going for different strategies. It is good to be open to new methods, but if the ways just spend your time or slow your progress, it is good to stick with what you know. Take time to modify what you have because that may be more beneficial for you as a trader. The art of mastering the industry involves that you deal with the little you know and work on it until perfection. When you have perfected one area, you can then pick another area and work on it. In short, it is good to subdivide your trading schedules and work on them individually than picking a big task that will not yield you much result.

Keep Practicing

It is good for a trader to first try by practicing to ensure that they are more comfortable in the market before investing their money. Practicing before you finally get to put your money will give you security because you already know what you are about to face. You may achieve this by using a trading simulator, which will help you get a feel of the real work awaiting you. When you finally are convinced that you are up to the task, then you can venture into trading. Then when you eventually become a trader, it is good to keep putting into practice all the different methods you learn along the way. Every opportunity as a trader should be used to perfect on your skills, and the way to perfecting is by ensuring that you are not lazy but keep learning.

Don't Be Too Excited

Excitement is good, but in trading, it will cost you a lot. You may be too excited and end up making rushed decisions that will make you losses. Sometimes the market works too much in your favor that you begin to think you are perfect. You may keep getting it right, but you still need to be careful because getting too excited may make you make a small mistake that will bring you down. Your strategy may be working, but that does not make you an overnight prophet that you now think your predictions are always right. You will still need to keep observing the market; you will still need to keep trying different strategies because there is no guarantee that you will keep winning. Losing several times, on the other hand, does not make you a definite failure. You don't have to keep taking bigger risks to ensure that you recover your money. Take your time and strategize your moves and see where you are going wrong instead of crucifying yourself. Do not be too hard on yourself simply because a few times the plan didn't work out for you. But also, do not let the excitement make you too overconfident as overconfident is most likely to bring you down. When you can seem to strike a balance, it is good to take a break from trading and relax. Continuing like this will be more harmful to you than if you had relaxed.

CHAPTER 15:

Building Up Your Watch List

As an active day trader, you must create a trading watch list. Basically, this is a list where you record the daily share prices of a group of stocks over time. It acts like a menu for the trading day. Based on the fundamental and technical new catalyst, a trading watch list should have active stocks that are ready to trade. It can either be done on the notepad, a spreadsheet, or even on paper. There are many software programs and other utilities that help in generating a watch list. It can also be provided by some brokerage houses where you pay a minimal charge, or for free.

A trader can have more than one watch list, but there are two specific watch lists that every active trader should never mess; a general watch list and a dynamic watch list. The general one may be composed of hundreds of stocks that are familiar to the trader. Every trader should also narrow down from the general watch list and come up with an active stock watch list every trading day before the market opening. This watch list should have stocks that the trader has been watching for days or weeks, that may be about to set up for a technical movement.

Stocks in Play

When a stock is widely believed to be a takeover target, it is said to be in play. Day traders widely trade stocks in play because their volatility produces reasonable risks and trading opportunities. When company stocks have less volatility, they move slowly, and they only have a reasonable price change only when the company shows good or bad trading outcomes. This may occur only a few times in a year. Such companies are ideal for investors looking for returns in the long-term. Long term investors buy shares in these companies, which have good prospects, with shares moving slowly in the right direction, and it matters less to them if the share price doesn't move much intraday. But day traders buy and sell stocks during stock market opening hours and exit the trade before the day ends. Sometimes they even trade for a few minutes or an hour and exit the market. They, therefore, require more action than investors. They need stocks that move and produce price swings so that their trade becomes worthwhile. Such fluctuations in prices leave enough room for them to realize profits, after paying the association fees charged by stockbrokers for buying and selling shares.

Stocks in play also have a large volume. Day traders are after quick entries and exits, and they want liquid stocks. That means they can buy and sell shares in the stock on demand. The broker is unable to negotiate the deal that the trader wants to buy or sell at. For day traders, this is a problem because it means the difference between a profitable trade and a non-profitable one. Day traders are guided by trade volumes of shares that are traded each day to arrive at what they consider good liquidity for them. For most traders, one hundred thousand shares traded per day would be their minimum, while some other traders may require a million shares.

Stocks in play will change in one day. An ordinary stock will be put in play by the company news which is typically released early in the morning, and it will vary depending on the nature of the news, whether it is good or bad.

Float and Market Cap

As an active day trader, it is crucial to understand the link between company size, risk, and return potential. Such information is vital as you lay the foundation to pursue long-term trading goals. With such knowledge, you can build a balanced watch list that comprises different market caps.

Market cap means market capitalization. It expresses the stock value of all the company shares. To arrive at the market cap of an entity, multiply the entities' shares by the stock price. An Entity with $50 million in shares with each share trading at $20 then $10 billion will be its market cap. Market cap is necessary because it helps traders to understand and compare the size of different companies. Market cap helps you to know the worth of different companies in the open market. It also helps you to understand how the market perceives a particular company and mirrors what investors and traders are ready to pay for its stock.

Large-cap stocks: $10 billion and over is their stock market value. Typically, these are reputable companies that produce quality goods and services. They experience steady growth and have a history of consistency in dividend payments to their shareholders. Their brand names are familiar to national and even international consumer audience. They are dominant players in their respective industries of the establishment. They are ideal for conservative investors since they pose less risk as they have less growth potential.

Mid-cap stocks: Typically, these are businesses with a minimum market value of $2 billion and a maximum market value of $10 billion. In other words, their market value is between $2 billion and $10 billion. They are medium-sized, established companies with growth potential. Such companies are either experiencing rapid growth, or there is an expectation that they will grow rapidly in the near future. They are in the stage of boosting their competitive advantage and widening their share of the market. This is a crucial stage since it determines their ability to attain maximum potential. In terms of risk, they have less risk in comparison with new startups. When it comes to potential, they offer more potential than blue-chip companies since they are expected to continue to grow until they reach full potential.

Small caps: their market stock value ranges from $300 million to $2 billion. They are growing businesses that are just emerging in the industry. They are the riskiest and the most aggressive and rely on niche marketing to survive in the industry. Due to limited resources, they are vulnerable to economic shocks. They are susceptible to intense competition and market uncertainties. Since they are new startups, they have high growth potential in the long-term, and they are ideal for investors who can cope up with volatile stock price swings in the short-run.

Float, on the other hand, is the number of shares, which are available for trading by the general public. Unlike the market cap that calculates the total stock value of all company shares, free-float does not include locked-in shares. Locked-in shares are those that are held by company employees and the government.

Pre-Market Gappers

Pre-market trading refers to trading activities that take place between 8 am and 9:30 am EST every trading day. This is usually before the regular market session begins. Traders and investors monitor the pre-market trading period to judge the direction and the strength of the market while waiting for the regular trading session. During the pre-market activity, there is limited liquidity and volume. Wide bid-ask spreads is a common thing during the pre-market period. The type of orders that can be used during this period is limited by many retail brokers, even though they offer pre-market trading. As early as 4 am, direct-access brokers begin to allow access to the pre-market activity to start. It is crucial to bear in mind that there is a limited activity during this pre-market period.

Real-Time Intraday Scans

A stock scanner is a screening tool that uses user-selected criteria and trading metrics to search the market and find stocks that meet the set standards. They can be modified to find the most suitable candidates that match user-specific filters using technology. They have helped to streamline the time-consuming task of attempting to trace new trading opportunities. This makes it efficient and convenient for traders to quickly find potential stocks. It is an essential tool for traders and investors due to its speed and convenience.

Real-time intraday scans are essential for day traders, and they work to spot stocks during market hours. They produce results that are highly sensitive to time and require the trader to analyze them quickly on the fly to determine whether a trade should be made. Intraday patterns require quick action as they develop and fade within a short period. Real-time intraday scans help day traders to maximize the limited time duration they have to make decisions before the patterns shift. They are a great way to introduce a trader to new stocks, especially when they search the whole market for candidates. These new stocks can then be added to the watch list. These new stocks can then be monitored to get acclimated to the liquidity, trade volume, spread, and the pace of the price action. A trader can dramatically narrow his field by modifying the filters to search only for stocks that meet his desired price range and minimum volume requirements.

CHAPTER 16:

Economic Factors Influencing Investment Prospects

Take a quick look at the headlines in the world's newspapers today and you'll see that huge events happen all the time. As a general rule, anything that causes fear and uncertainty is going to have a significant impact on the Forex market – and on your own individual trades, too. You can't see most of them coming, but you can prepare.

These massive events can include natural disasters such as earthquakes, hurricanes, conflict from wars or terrorism events, and human-created disasters such as the meltdown of a nuclear reactor.

It's not uncommon for a country to shut down its markets when a massive event happens for the simple reason that panic can often lead to a crash. It's a way to ensure that cooler heads prevail before disaster strikes the financial markets.

When the market is shut, there's nothing you can do about your trades — they are frozen for the duration and your orders will not be fulfilled. The best way to avoid this from having a severe effect on your capital is to make sure you always leave stop-loss orders to automatically protect your position even when you can't do so yourself.

There are myriad influences on the market and they're all happening constantly, each one pushing the market up and down of their own accord while remaining just one part of the spider web and thus influenced in turn by other influences. Some of these influencers have global impacts and some will only affect certain aspects of a single country.

Option Expirations

Be aware that funny things can happen on the monthly and quarterly expiration dates for the options market. Sellers will be aiming to secure certain price levels, which means volatility that can have a knock-on effect. Avoid these dates for new trades.

Statements from Officials

When officials from governments and banks make statements about the economy and financial situation, it can hold great weight with the marketplace. Watch out for press releases and even the minutes from meetings, as these can change the marketplace almost instantly, especially if they imply changes and movements that had not been foreseen.

Business Activities

When huge companies deal internationally, there is always a need for currency exchange. To acquire assets, even make big trading deals, one partner will need to exchange their local currency to pay the other partner. This temporarily changes how much cash is available in either currency, affecting demand and supply.

Market Ratings

Certain financial service companies are tasked with analyzing a country's finances and rating them accordingly. A triple-A rating ("AAA") means that the country has the capacity to meet its financial commitments; the lower the rating, the less they are believed able to do this. When ratings are released, they can significantly impact the economy of the country. A downgrade will have a negative impact, while an upgrade will have a positive impact.

Interventions

We've mentioned already that central banks in certain countries can be a lot more hands-on than in others. In truth, most central banks are willing to get involved if the currency is spiraling in one direction or the other, though some more than others. It's worth knowing how hands-on the central banks are in the countries you'll be dealing with, because an intervention will adjust the volatility and impact the currency dramatically.

Political Changes

The markets don't like uncertainty, and a change in leadership is very much a time of uncertainty. When a country votes in a new administration, it's impossible to be sure who will win that election and what policies they will aim to fulfill. For the most part, you'll find that the volatility increases for that currency while the election is ongoing and for a certain amount of time afterward, until the new administration has made its intentions clear.

The Bond Market

The bond market is a huge piece of the financial marketplace and, as such, has a big impact on trends in currencies. Informed traders like to stay abreast of what's happening in the bond market because the way money flows in and out of it correlates with what's happening in the currency market and can be very influential in pushing trends.

Monetary Policies

Central banks handle interest rates and the supply of money. Policies are used to maintain control over inflation and make sure the currency remains as stable as possible. It's arguably much easier to keep an eye on these policies and predict what they will do to the market because they are aimed directly at the markets, so they have clear aims that will have clearer effects on your trades.

Government Policies

Laws and regulations that a government puts in place can have a significant impact on the market. The objective of these policies tend to be directed towards keeping prices stable, making sure employment levels are as high as possible and promoting the economy. Be aware that there are many tools a government can employ to influence what's happening to the economy, from new tax policies to a policy that aims to increase business activities.

Analyzing an Economy

The many economies of the world are in a constant state of flux. You now know where to look to find out where in a cycle they currently are —and make trading decisions accordingly— but what do those cycles actually mean?

When boiled down to the basics, an economy is either going to be in a time of expansion or a time of recession. In the former case, there is an increase in economic activity and gross domestic product, which means more disposable income and thus spending, better employment levels and more demand.

A recession is basically the opposite and will see a drop in economic activity that has a blanket effect across internal markets for such things as housing and labor. If this gets bad enough or goes on for long enough, it becomes known as a depression.

Within those cycles you'll find inflation and deflation. Inflation refers to the prices being charged for items and services and usually rises when there is more demand than supply. Deflation, once again, is its opposite.

Gross domestic product refers to the overall value of those items and services that a single country generates over the course of one year. It's what the central banks tend to use to analyze the growth of the economy, which means it's also the best place to look to find out whether that country's economy is on the rise or on the decline.

It represents how much consumers are consuming, how much investment and government spending is going on and how much exporting is taking place.

Meanwhile, the "balance of payments" can tell you how healthy the economy is in comparison to others in the world, and it can do so fairly directly. It refers to all international activities and is considered to be in a good state when the country is accepting more payments from other countries than it is making.

The financial account will tell you how many international assets the country owns by looking at change in ownership. The country's budget deficit —the amount it must borrow above its income from taxes to meet the needs of its budget— will also indicate its internal economic health.

In general, what all these things will tell you is how risky the market is at the current moment. An economic decline is a time for safe bets, so it's usually when you'll find traders turning their attention to those safe currencies. In a time of increase, they will look more towards riskier currencies, which include the Canadian dollar, the Australian dollar, the New Zealand dollar, the British pound, and the Euro.

CHAPTER 17:

Effective Methods for Manage Your Money

T he truth is that many traders, especially novices, started with a lot in their trading accounts, and at the end of the day, they had little or nothing to boast. Many of them lost their funds because of thoughtless actions or not following a well-crafted strategy. There are some things that you have to do to manage your money well.

Choose the Right Lot Size Based on Your Capital

When you start at forex training or financial market trading, you will tend to learn about trading lots. What we mean by a lot is the tiniest trade size available that can be placed when you decide to trade currency pairs on the foreign exchange market.

Usually, brokers tend to talk about lots using increments of a thousand or a micro lot. You have to understand that the lot size determines directly, as well as shows that risk among that you are willing to take.

Using a risk management calculator or a top like that can help you know the right lot size, based on what your trading account assets are currently. This can be used when you are trading life, or you are merely practicing. It allows you to know what amount that can be risked.

The trading lot size affects how the market movements can affect the accounts. Let's use an example.

When a 100-pip move occurs, it won't have so much effect on a small trade like a similar 100-pip move on a trade size that is quite massive.

As a trader, you will see several lot sizes.

We will explain the lots as follow:

Trading with Micro Lots

The tiniest tradable lots that can be used are called mini lots. A micro lot has a thousand units of the currency that is in your account. If you have funded your account with USD, a micro-lot of that has a value of a thousand dollars, as the base currency.

If you have decided to trade a dollar-based pair, a pip means ten cents.

As a beginner, it is favorable to use micro-lots to reduce your risk while you practice trading.

Mini lots have ten thousand units of the currency that you use to fund your account. If you are making use of an account with dollars as its base currency, then every pip in the trade would be valued at around $1.00.

As a beginner that wants to begin with mini lots, you should be adequately capitalized.

A dollar per pip may seem quite tiny, but the market sometimes gets to a hundred pips daily. Sometimes, this may happen in one hour.

If the forex market isn't moving in your direction, this means that you have made a loss of a hundred dollars.

It is you that will choose your ultimate risk tolerance. Before you can trade a mini account, you shouldn't mind using at least two thousand dollars.

Using Standard Lots

A standard lot has a hundred thousand units of the base currency in a trading account. If you have a base currency of dollars, this is a hundred thousand dollar lots. The normal pip size for a standard lot is ten dollars for every pip.

When the trade is against you by ten pip, this is a loss of hundred dollars. Institutional-sized accounts use this type of lot.

What this translates to is that you should possess at least $25,000 to be able to carry out trades using standard lots.

A lot of forex traders tend to make use of either micro-lots or mini lots.

To a novice, this may not seem glamorous, but when you keep the lot size proportional to your account's size, your trading capital will be preserved, and you can easily trade with it for a long while.

Let's use an illustration;

Using a small trade size compared to what you have in your account can be likened to strolling on a sturdy bridge with a shelter to prevent any issue from worrying you. It doesn't matter if heavy rain occurs; you will be sheltered.

If you place a big trade size compared to the account funds, it can be likened to walking on a narrow bridge. In this case, the bridge is fragile and narrow, meaning that you can fall. A tiny movement in the market could toss you away and lead you to a spot that you can't return from.

Below are some things you should consider before you begin.

Do not let your gain become a loss

One thing that has been noticed is that many forex traders tend to turn their profit into a loss. The forex market worldwide does at least $5 trillion daily. This has made it the most significant financial market globally.

The fact that Forex is lucrative has made it popular amongst many traders from novices to experts in the field.

Since it is quite easy to get involved in Forex because of the little costs, round-the-clock sessions, and so on, it is also straightforward to lose your capital as you trade Forex.

To ensure that your gain doesn't turn to a loss as a forex trader, you should try and avoid some mistakes.

Learn, Learn and Learn

The fact that it is quite easy to get involved in Forex has led many people to get involved without bothering to learn. To succeed in Forex or any financial market for that matter, you need to learn. You should learn from live trading, experience, as well as reading up on forex literature. Don't forget the news. You spiel find out about economic and geopolitical factors that affect the preferred currencies of a trader.

The world of Forex is ever-changing, meaning that you must keep yourself abreast of these changes in the regulations, market conditions, as well as global events.

While you undergo the research process, you should also consider creating a trading plan.

This plan should involve a method where you can screen and analyze investments in a bid to determine how much risk should be expected when creating investment goals.

Use only a reputable broker

The truth is that the forex world isn't so regulated, unlike others, meaning that you may end up carrying out business with unscrupulous brokers. It is advisable that you only open an account with a National Futures Association (NFA) member if you want your deposits to be safe. You are interested in the integrity of that broker. Use only brokers that are listed as futures commission merchant with the regulatory body of your country. If the broker isn't registered, avoid them.

It is also advisable that you study the brokers' account offerings like commissions, leverage amounts, spreads, account withdrawal, funding policies, and so on. You can find these out by talking to a customer service representative.

Utilize a practice account

Almost every trading platform out there has a practice account. This is also called a demo account or a simulated account.

The account permits traders to carry out hypothetical trades that do not need a funded account. Using a perceive account allows the trader to get used to order-entry techniques quickly.

Using a practice account allows the trader to learn, thereby avoiding a lot of mistakes in their trading account.

We had seen cases of when a novice trader erroneously adds to a losing position when he intended to close the trade.

Several errors in the order entry could worsen to a big losing trade. Losing funds is not the only issue; you have to also battle with a stressful and annoying situation.

There is nothing wrong if you decide to try out order entries before you start to place the real money on live trading.

Keep Your Charts clean

When a forex trader creates an account, he or she may be tempted to use every tech assessment tool available in the trading platform.

Many of these indicators are high in the foreign exchange market, but you should reduce the hunger of analysis methods you use to be efficient.

You are making use of several similar indicators like three oscillators, or as three volatility indicators may come off as unnecessary. Sometimes, you may even get opposite signals. You should try and avoid this.

If you aren't using an analysis technique well, consider taking it out of your chart. It is also essential that you look at the total appearance of the workspace.

The hues, kinds, and fonts of price hard such as candle bar, line, range bar, and so on that you use should craft out an easy-to-read-and-interpret chart, permitting you to respond to the ever-changing conditions in the market quickly.

Stop Loss Order Is Not Just for Preventing Losses

Stop-loss orders are used a lot in preventing losses, but it does more than that. It can also be used in locking profits. If used for this, it is sometimes called a "trailing stop."

At this point, the stop-loss order is being set at a percent height that is beneath the current market price and different from the price that it was bought.

The stop loss's price fluctuates the same way the price of the stock adjusts.

This means that if the price of a stock increases, you may have to battle with an unrealized gain. This means that you won't have the money with you until after the sales.

Making use of trailing stop permits you to allow your run, and still guarantee you an amount of realized capital gain.

You must note that the stop-loss order will always be a market order, meaning that it would lie low until the trigger price has been reached. This means that the price your stock may sell for may end up being a bit different from what you specified as your trigger price.

Benefits of stop-loss order

One thing that we all love about stop loss is the fact that we don't have to pay a dime to implement it. The normal commission is only charged when you have reached a stop-loss price, and your stock has been sold. What you should see it as is a free insurance policy.

Using a stop loss ensured decisions are made based on facts and taking out any form of emotional influence.

Many people end up crushing on their stocks, feeling that if they allowed the stock to stay on, it would surely succeed, even when the facts are saying another story. This leads to delay and procrastination on the part of the trader, and before you know it, he is raking in unimaginable losses.

It doesn't matter what kind of trader you see yourself as; there must be a reason you have decided to own a stock.

The criteria listed by a value investor is usually different from the one listed by a growth investor and an active trader.

CHAPTER 18:

Trading Strategies for Beginners

Many make the error of thinking that you need a highly convoluted strategy for intraday success. Still, the suggestion is to always go with the simplest of the solutions and ideas.

Apart from all the vital factors, you should also incorporate these below mentioned essential components into your approach.

- **Money Management**

Sit downward and find out how much you're prepared to drop before you initiate. Keep in mind that most effectual traders would not place more than 2 percent of their wealth per trade on the ground. If you want to be around when the wins' start progressing in, you have to support yourself for some defeats.

- **Time Management**

Don't plan to create a fortune if you're just assigning an hour or two a day to trade. You have to trail the markets always and be on the lookout for trade opportunities.

- **Start Low**

Stick to the greatest of three stocks during a single day when you're finding your feet. It's much better to get good at a few than being mediocre and not making cash on lots.

- **Education**

Knowing the intricacies of the market isn't enough, you need to keep updated. Make sure you stay up-to-date with market reports and any developments that affect your properties, such as a financial policy change. You will find a diversity of financial and business tools online, which will keep you in the circle.

- **Consistency**

It's easier than it appears when you're five coffees in, and you've been staring at the computer for hours to keep thoughts in the bay. You need to be motivated by math, logic, and your preparation, not by nervousness, fear, or greed.

- **Timing**

As it opens every day, the market can turn out to be changeable, and although experienced day traders will be intelligent to read the trends and advantages, you should propose your time. But grasp on for the first 15 minutes, and you still have hours in front of you.

- **Demo Account**

A must has source for any beginner, but also the perfect position to the backrest or play with new or complicated, advanced traders strategies. Many demo accounts are unobstructed, so feel free to have one.

Breakout

Breakout strategies focus around when the cost on your chart reaches a defined level, with an augmented volume. After the benefit or security breaks above confrontation, the breakout trader enters a great arrangement. Alternatively, if the stock falls below to hold up, you'll reach a little spot.

Following an asset or commodity trades above the defined price limit, volatility characteristically rises, and prices regularly trend towards running away.

You need to discover the right instrument for the trade. Bear in the brain the level of hold up and resistance of the asset when doing so. The more often those points have been smacked by the market, the more they are validated and essential.

Entry Points

This part is pleasant and straightforward. Prices set to close up, and higher rates of confrontation warrant a bearish role. Prices set to close and need an optimistic place below the support level.

Plan your Exits

Make use of the up to date performance of the asset to set a sensible price target. Using chart trends will intensify this cycle even more. To create a goal, you can work out the average recent price swings. If the standard price change over the last few market fluctuations has been 3 points, which would be an evenhanded target. Once that objective reaches, you can exit the trade and enjoy the advantage.

Scalping

Scalping is one of the most comprehensive strategies. In the forex market, it is particularly common, and it looks like capitalizing on minute price changes. The foundation is quantity. As soon as the trade is money-making, you can search for sales. It is an exhilarating and fast-paced way to trade, but it can be hazardous. To balance out the low-risk/recompense ratio, you need a high trading possibility.

Search for aggressive products, be profitable in liquidity, and be hot on time. You can't wait for the financial system; you have to close your losing trades as rapidly as you can.

Momentum

This strategy, which is familiar amongst trading strategies for starters, revolves around acting on news sources and identifying significant tendency movements with the help of high dimensions. There's always at least one stock moving around 20-30 percent each day, so demand is abundant. You just hang on to your place until you see signs of spinning back and then get out.

On the other hand, the price drop will fade. It rounds off your price objective as soon as quantity starts to diminish. If used properly, the strategy is straightforward and efficient. You must also make sure you are aware of approaching notifications of news and earnings. Just a small number of seconds on any trade will make all variation to your earnings at the end of the day.

Reversal

Although powerfully and potentially hazardous when used by beginners, reverse trading used wide-reaching. It is also known as pattern trading, trending pulls back, and a mean reversal strategy.

This strategy defies simple logic because you are trying to trade the pattern back. You require being able to recognize the potential pullbacks accurately, plus predict their power. To do so effectively, you need detailed knowledge and understanding of the business.

The 'daily reversal' strategy considered a special reverse trading occasion because it focuses on buying and selling the low and high pullbacks/reverse each day regularly.

Using Pivot Points

A pivot point line of attack for day trading can be overwhelming to be familiar with and operate on vital support and resistance rates. It is predominantly useful in the forex market. Additionally, range-bound traders can use it to describe entry points, while trend and breakout traders can use to activate points to find key levels that need to break to meet the criteria as a breakout for a jump.

CHAPTER 19:

Advanced Day Trading Strategies

W hen you are looking forward to capitalizing on the small frequent price movements, day trading strategies are the best for you. Any effective strategy that you will choose must be consistent and must rely on in-depth technical analysis that utilizes charts, market patterns and price indicators predicting future price movements.

It is your responsibility to choose the most appropriate strategy that best fits your requirements. As a trader, it is good that you know the average daily trading volume.

Fallen Angel

A Fallen Angel is a strategy that involves a bond that has been reduced to junk bond status from an investment-grade rating as a result of the issuer's weakening financial conditions. In terms of stock, a fallen angel refers to a stock that has always been high and now has fallen considerably. Fallen angel bonds can be a sovereign, corporate or municipal debt that a rating service has downgraded. The main reason for such downgrades could be attributed to revenue decline that generally jeopardizes the capabilities of issuers to servicing debt. The potential for downgrade often experiences a dramatic increase when expanding debts are combined with expanding debt levels. The securities of fallen angels are at times so attractive, particularly to contrarian investors who seek to capitalize on the potential. This enables the issuer to recover from the temporary setback.

Example

Due to the ever-falling oil prices over several quarters, an oil company has reported sustained losses. The company, therefore, can decide to downgrade its investment-grade bonds to junk status as a result of the increasing risk of default. This will result in a decline in the prices of the company's bonds and as well increase yields thus, this will make the contrarian investors to be attracted to the debt as they only see the low oil prices as a temporary condition. However, there are conditions where you are likely to go at a loss especially when the fallen angel bond issuers do not recover. For example, is there is an introduction of superior products by a rival company, the issuers may fail to recover.

ABCD Pattern / Reverse ABCD Pattern

The ABCD pattern is a pattern that shows perfect harmony between price and time. ABCD pattern usually reflects the common and rhythmic style on the market movements. The geometric price/time pattern consists of three consecutive price trends with a leading indicator that can guide a trader to determine when and where to enter and exit a trade. As a trader, ABCD Pattern can be very important in identifying the available trading opportunities in any market (be it futures, forex or stock) on any timeframe (be its position, intraday or swing), and in any market condition (be it range-bound, bullish or bearish markets). Before placing a trade, ABCD Pattern can help you determine the reward and the risks of trade.

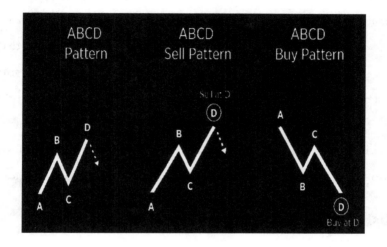

Fig. 1: A representation of the ABCD Pattern (Above)

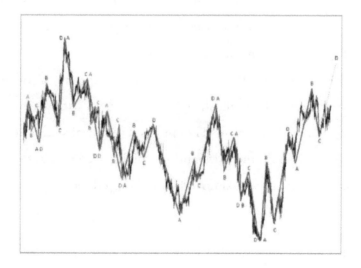

Fig. 2: ABCD pattern on a trading chart

Bull Flag and Bear Flag

With technical analysis, a flag refers to a price pattern that can explode and move within a shorter timeframe to the prevailing price trend that has always been observed in longer time frames on a price chart. With the flag patterns, a trader can identify the possible prevailing a trend that is continuing from a given point where the price has drifted against the same trend. Therefore, in the case that the trend resumes, by noticing the flag pattern, there will be a rapid price increase and this makes the timing of a trade advantageous. Flags are areas of tight consolidation in price actions and they show a counter-trend sharp directional movement in price. This pattern has 5 to 20 price bars.

Bullish Flag Formation

These are formation patterns observed in stocks that have a strong uptrend. Bull flags got their names from the fact that the pattern closely resembles a flag on a pole. A vertical rise in-stock results to a pole and a period of consolidation results to a flag. The flag is usually angled down away from the trend that is prevailing but also can be a horizontal rectangle. The bullish flag pattern starts with a strong price spike that is almost vertical. The prices then peaks and forms an orderly pullback where the lows and the highs become almost parallel to each other making them almost to form a tilted rectangle.

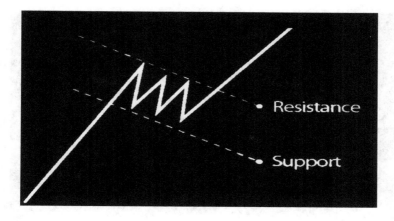

Fig 3: Bullish Flag Formation

The parallel diagonal nature is reflected by the plotted trendlines (both lower and upper trendlines). The breaking of the upper resistance trend line forms the first breakout. Another uptrend move and a breakout are formed when there is an explosion of the prices, causing prices to surge back towards the high of the formation.

Bearish Flag

Comparing to the bullish flag, this flag is an upside-down version of the bull flag. The bearish flag is an inverted version of the bull flag. In this case, an almost vertical panic price drop is formed by the flagpole because the sellers make the bulls to get blindsided and, as a result, there is a bounce having a parallel lower and upper trendlines, forming the flag. The panic sellers are triggered when the lower trendlines break. This flag is similar to the bull flag in that the severity of the drop on the flagpole will determine how the strength the bear flag can be.

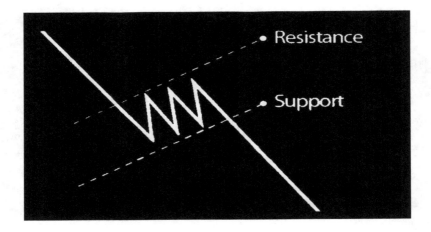

Fig. 4: The Bearish flag

Develop Trading Skills

To become a trader, you are required to not only know about just finance or business but also in hard science or mathematics. You must be an individual who can do deep research and analysis that can mirror the economic factors from a broader perspective as well as the day-to-day chart patterns impacting on different financial markets. As a trader, it is crucial that you need to sharpen your ability to concentrate and focus, especially in a fast-moving environment containing different people with different goals and ideas. You must also be able to practice self-control and regulate your emotions even when in situations upsetting you. Lastly, you should always be able to keep an accurate record of your trades to check on your account and to provide you with a learning opportunity that will help you become a better trader.

CHAPTER 20:

Controlling Emotions After a Loss

Do Not Take Huge Risks

Avoid greed at all cost when it comes to day trading. Before taking any risk, look at the possibility of losing the money. If you cannot cope with the possibility of losing, then it is not worth investing your money. Always keep in mind that even with the best strategies, the chances of winning investment in a stock market is 50/50. Also, take time to learn the exact ratios that apply in the stock market since they fluctuate from time to time.

Don't Invest with The Intention of Revenge

As a human being, you are likely to respond to an inevitable failure with a vengeance. Never approach day trade with such plan since you are likely to fail terribly. In case of a failure, sit back and study to know the cause of your failures. Take time to strategize your move. I can assure you that getting into the market an intention of revenge will cause you more harm than good.

Do Not Trade Too Many Times

You should trade once in a while. Only put on an investment when an excellent opportunity presents itself. Proper analysis is essential before putting your money on any stock market. However, you can spend as much time as you can analyze the market situation instead of doing the actual trading. Quit spending too much time trading since it is a recipe for disaster.

Do Not Scalp If You Are New in the Market

Scalping is merely taking a short cut by taking on trades that last only for a few seconds. Even though scalping is the right way of making good money, it is precarious. You need a certain level of skill and experience to understand and predict a sudden shift in market movements. In every trade you take, you required to pay spread fee notwithstanding the direction taken by any trade. Therefore, experience and knowledge are essential since you have got to achieve pips above the spread cost.

It is essential to take notes as you try different strategies. Stock marketplace, experience, and knowledge are the two most important factors.

Do Not Trust Unreliable Sources of Information

Often you receive emails, text messages or advertisements claiming a good profit on any stocks. Not that you shut down such sources, ensure the information they give is authentic and reliable. As a good trader, be careful not to fall into the hands of brokers who are hungry for commotions. These people can easily land you into bad trade hence losses.

Keep Away from Penny Stocks

As a starter in day trading, penny stocks should be the last thing you should do. Experienced traders will tell you that you should not engage in a trade that is difficult to exit. Also, penny stocks are highly illiquid; hence your chances of hitting huge profits are low.

Do Not Refuse to Take Out Your Profits

It natural for any human being to want more or never get satisfied with whatever they have since everyone is in business to make an extra coin. Moreover, a mistake comes in when you want to make quick money. As a result, every trader wants to make unimaginable profits with their first trade. However, in the stock market, which looks like a huge gain could end up to be a huge loss. Well, expecting a huge increase in your trade is not bad. However, it is essential to be realistic about the kind of profits you expect from your investment.

Winning vs. Losing in Day trading

Most people follow the world of online trading closely. Interestingly, some of these people never invest in trading. Well, it is not a bad thing to follow and understand how trading could impact your financial goals. However, you also need to realize that there are benefits of trying out the idea of trading. Win or lose; there is something important which you will learn from the activity. So, if you have never traded before, you shouldn't be afraid to try. After all, there is no harm in trying. Keep in mind that various brokers will help you initiate your trading activity without having to use your funds. It is made possible by using free demo accounts.

Knowing that there is something in store for you, whether you win or lose in day trading, should motivate you in taking the right steps to become a trader. Traders who have been in business for some time will argue that there is a rewarding feeling in learning something from an exciting activity like day trading. Some life lessons which you will learn in the process of trading briefly tackle in the following lines.

Enhanced Decision Making

Online trading requires one to develop a sound decision-making process as this will lead to the best results. By constantly finding a way to improve the decision-making process, a trader also increases their chances of earning good returns. The notion of doing this will ultimately have a positive impact on one's life. When a trader seeks to improve how well they make their decisions, they also end up affecting their day to day decisions. It means that the quality of life of any trader would considerably be improved.

Self-Awareness

With online trading, there is a guarantee that you will develop a sense of self-awareness you might have never had before. Trading with emotions will often cloud your judgment. For example, you might stay too long on a trade without selling out. Also, you could tempt to enter a trade just because you have nothing to do. You will incur losses because your decision-making process is clouded.

In real-life situations, there are many times when we blind from perceiving life with objectivity. Most of the decisions we end up making affect our personal lives. By choosing to learn how to succeed in day trading, you will also learn how to make sound decisions in life without allowing your emotions to come in the way. The best part is that you will also learn how to appreciate things the way they are. Simply stated, this is the kind of personality that day trading requires any trader.

Entrepreneurship Skills

Interestingly, the skills you obtain while day trading could apply in other businesses that you might be running. To succeed in business, you need to know the existence of risks which could negatively affect your business. Similarly, you need to learn how to mitigate such risks using feasible solutions. When you choose to engage in online trading, you get all these lessons for free. The strategies you employ to lower your risks can use to ensure that your businesses always thrive. So, as earlier mentioned, whether you succeed or fail in day trading, there is something good you will be taking home.

Uncertainty Is Your Closest Friend

Nothing is guaranteed when engaging in online trading. Markets can move in any direction. Therefore, you could either make profits or losses depending on how you predicted the markets to perform. In real-life situations, there is nothing we are always sure. Whether you are opening a new business or taking on a new venture, you have never tried before, and it is all about uncertainty. Trading in securities over the internet will help you a mentality where you accept that uncertainty is your closest friend.

Taking Risks and Reducing Risk

Most people are afraid to try online trading because of its associated risks. A common myth you will hear from traders who have failed is that day trading is too risky and unprofitable. It is not the case. You will only lose on day trading when you fail to implement the best strategies. For instance, you need to have a risk mitigation strategy as well as an overall trading strategy. Knowing how to stomach huge risks with the anticipation of making profits is not easy. It is an art. Very few people are willing to take risks in their lives. It is the number one reason why most entrepreneurs fail. Choosing not to take a risk can prove to be costly. It is because one might end up losing out in an opportunity that would have transformed their lives. So, day trading will teach you a lot about taking risks and reducing risks.

Importance of Diversification

The phrase "you should not put all your eggs in one basket" applies to numerous life situations. Whether in business or your career, it is always important to diversify. Diversifying your activities prevents you from making huge losses, in business, diversifying guarantees that you make profits even when one of your businesses is not working out. For instance, if you are offering two products to the market, through diversification, you can be sure that one of the products will perform well. Day trading will teach you that it is essential to diversify as it

159

helps you spread your risks. Therefore, it is a valuable lesson for most people.

Looking Beyond Financial Gains

There are numerous times that you must have told to have passion in whatever you do. Well, this is true for most businesses. The only way that you will truly succeed in business in your career is by falling in love with what you do. Day trading will be the right training school. It will help you understand that it is more than just the money you are after. When trading using smaller accounts, your focus will be on getting experience and learning how to trade. Ideally, your aim is learning something new from the trading activity. Therefore, there is a rewarding feeling in knowing that you are a better trader today than yesterday. With this mentality, you will live to appreciate the idea of gaining experience from any activity you engage in. Hence, if you will be opening up a new store around the corner and it fails to succeed, you will be happy you tried and failed than failing to try ultimately.

I hope you see how day trading could impact your life in many ways. If you have the right mentality when you are entering any trading market, you will enjoy the activity over the long haul. Don't believe the hype that is out in the streets. Have confidence that your plan works despite the few losses here and there. As always, you should motivate yourself with the notion that even the most experienced of traders incur huge losses. So, before you think that day trading will not help you in any way, think twice.

CHAPTER 21:

Choose The Best Instruments to Day Trade

Trading in Stocks

The thought of trading in stocks scares away many investors. Individuals who have never traded are terrified by the fact that one can easily lose money with wrong decisions. The reality is stock trading is a risky activity. However, when approached with the right market knowledge, it is an efficient way of building your net worth.

So, what is a stock? A stock is a share. It is also termed as equity. Basically, it is a financial instrument which amounts to ownership in a company. When an individual purchase a stock or shares, it means that they own a portion or fraction of the company. For instance, say a trader own 10,000 shares in a company with 100,000 shares. This would mean that the individual has 10% ownership of the stakes. The buyer of such shares is identified as a shareholder. Therefore, the more shares one owns, the larger the proportion of the company which they own. Every time the value of the company shares rise, your share value will also rise. Similarly, if the value falls, your share value also declines. When a company makes a profit, the shareholders are also bestowed with the profits in the form of dividends.

Preferred stock and common stock are the two main types of stocks you should be aware of. The difference that lies between these stocks is that with common stocks, it carries voting rights. This means that a shareholder has an influence in company meetings. Hence, they can have a say in company meetings where the board of directors is elected. On the other hand, preferred shares lack voting rights. However, they are identified as "preferred" shares or stocks because of their preference over common stocks. In the event that a company goes through liquidation, shareholders with preferred shares will be preferred to receive assets or dividends.

Far from the information provided about the varying kinds of stock, a day trader doesn't necessarily have to understand the difference. Remember, you are only a day trader. Thus, you will only buy shares for a short period before selling them within the same day.

- **Capital Requirements**

According to the Pattern Day Trading Rule, the minimum brokerage balance you are required to maintain for you to trade in stocks is at least $25,000. Without a doubt, this is a lot of money to start with. Surprisingly, there are tons of traders who began with a lower amount than that. To understand how this rule applies, you need to know what it means to be a pattern day trader. This is the type of trader whereby they execute more than four traders within five business days in their margin accounts.

163

- **Leverage**

There are two ways of trading in stocks. You could either choose to trade using a margin account or a cash account. With the margin account, it gives a trader the opportunity of buying their stocks on margin. Conversely, with cash accounts, you only buy the stocks for the amount of money present in your account. In other words, you will be trading with a leverage ratio of 1:1.

The notion of trading on margin implies that you will be seeking for funds from your broker. This means that you will be able to buy more stocks far beyond what you can normally afford. To use a margin account, a trader will be required to have at least $2,000 as their starting capital. However, some brokers will demand more. Once your margin account is open, you can get a loan amounting to 50% of the buying price of the stock.

In a real-life example, say you make an initial deposit of $10,000 to your margin account. Since you deposited about 50% of the buying price, it means you are worth twice as much, i.e., $20,000. In other words, your buying power is worth twice what you deposited. Therefore, when you buy stocks worth $5,000, your buying power will reduce to $15,000. Your leverage ratio is, therefore, 1:2. Traders with a good trading relationship with their brokers could have this ratio increased to even 1:8.

- **Liquidity**

With regards to liquidity, you can be certain that trading in stocks is not a bad idea. There are over 10,000 stocks present in the U.S. stocks exchanges. Most of these stocks are traded on a daily basis. Dealing with these stocks guarantees that you evade the common issues of slippage or manipulation.

- **Volatility**

A trader shouldn't worry about the volatility of the stocks market as they often go through cycles of high and low. This is not a bad thing as a trader simply needs to study when the markets are rising and be wary of instances when markets seem to fall.

Trading in Forex

Most traders would argue that trading in forex is quite complicated. However, it's not. Just like any other form of trading, you have to stick to the basic rules. In this case, you need to buy when the market is rising and ensure you sell when the market is dropping. Basically, trading in forex involves the process of trading in currencies. In simpler terms, a trader exchanges currency for others based on certain agreed rates. If you have traveled to foreign countries and exchanged your currency against their local currencies, then you should understand how trading in forex works.

At first, it could seem confusing to choose the best currencies, but a trader should simply go for major currencies. Some of the frequently traded currencies include the U.S. dollar, Japanese Yen, European

Union Euro, Australian dollar, Canadian dollar, and Swiss franc. An important thing you ought to understand about forex trading is that you need to trade in pairs. This means that when you are buying one currency, you should do this while simultaneously selling another. If you do some digging, you will notice that currencies are quoted in pairs, i.e., USD/JPY or EUR/USD. Below is an image showing how currencies are quoted in pairs.

Often, the most traded forex products include:

- USD/JPY
- EUR/USD
- GBP/USD

An important thing to keep in mind with regards to forex trading is that the market is highly volatile. This means that a trader could easily lose a lot of money within a single day. Before venturing into this market, a trader should take time to understand this market in detail.

Trading in Futures

Today, most traders prefer to trade in futures due to its associated advantages. Trading in futures is quite flexible and diverse. The good news is that a trader can employ almost any methodology to trade. Some traders shy away from this form of trading due to their limited knowledge about futures. Also, others are discouraged from trading in futures because they think that it is difficult. Well, to some extent, this is true. Comparing trading in futures to trading in stocks, the former is very risky.

There are different forms of futures contracts including currencies, energies, interest rates, metals, food sector futures, and agricultural futures.

- **S&P 500 E-mini**

Most traders will fancy the idea of trading in the S&P 500 E-mini because of its high liquidity aspect. It also appeals to most investors because of its low day trading margins. You can conveniently trade in S&P 500 E-mini around the clock not to mention that you will also benefit from its technical analysis aspect. Essentially, the S&P 500 E-mini is a friendly contract since you can easily predict its price patterns.

- **10 Year T-Notes**

10 Year T-Notes is also ranked as one of the best contracts to trade in. Considering its sweet maturity aspect, most traders would not hesitate to trade in this futures contract. There are low margin requirements that a trader will have to meet when trading in 10 Year T-Notes.

- **Crude Oil**

Crude oil also stands as one of the most popular commodities in futures trading. It is an exciting market because of its high daily trading volume of about 800k. Its high volatility also makes the market highly lucrative.

- **Gold**

This is yet another notable futures contract. It might be expensive to trade in gold; however, it is a great hedging choice more so in poor market conditions.

CHAPTER 22:

Common Day Trading Mistakes to Avoid

Aside from doing the right things, you'll also need to refrain from certain things to succeed as a day trader. Following are some of the most common day trading mistakes you should avoid committing.

Excessive Day Trading

By excessive, I mean executing too many day trades. One of the most common mistakes many newbie day traders make is assuming that they can become day trading ninjas in just a couple of weeks if they trade often enough to get it right. But while more practice can eventually translate into day trading mastery in the future, it doesn't mean you can cram all that practice in a very short period of time via very frequent day trading. The adage "the more, the merrier" doesn't necessarily apply to day trading.

Remember, timing is crucial for day trading success. And timing is dependent on how the market is doing during the day. There will be days when day trading opportunities are few and far between and there'll be days when day trading opportunities abound. Don't force trades for the sake of getting enough day trades under your belt.

Even in the midst of a plethora of profitable day trading opportunities, the more, the merrier still doesn't apply. Why? If you're a newbie trader, your best bet at becoming a day trading ninja at the soonest possible time is to concentrate on one or two day trades per day only. By limiting your day trades, to just one or two, you have the opportunity to monitor and learn from your trades closely.

Can you imagine executing 5 or more trades daily as a newbie and monitor all those positions simultaneously? You'll only get confused and overwhelmed and worse, you may even miss day trading triggers and signals and fail to close your positions profitably.

Winging It

If you want to succeed as a day trader, you need to hold each trading day in reverence and high esteem. Plan your day trading strategies for the day and execute those strategies instead of just winging it.

As cliché as it may sound, failing to plan really is planning to fail. And considering the financial stakes involved in day trading, you shouldn't go through your trading days without any plan on hand. Luck favors those who are prepared and planning can convince lady luck that you are prepared.

Expecting Too Much Too Soon

This much is true about day trading: it's one of the most exciting and exhilarating jobs in the world! And stories many day traders tell of riches accumulated through this economic activity add more excitement, desire, and urgency for many to get into it.

However, too much excitement and desire resulting from many day trading success stories can be very detrimental to newbie day traders. Let me correct myself: it is detrimental to newbie day traders. Why?

Such stories, many of which are probably urban legends, give newbies unrealistic expectations of quick and easy day trading riches. Many beginner day traders get the impression that day trading is a get-rich-quick scheme!

It's not. What many day traders hardly brag about are the times they also lost money and how long it took them to master the craft enough to quit their jobs and do it full time. And even rarer are stories of the myriad number of people who've attempted day trading and failed. It's the dearth of such stories that tend to make day trading neophytes have unrealistic expectations about day trading.

What's the problem with lofty day trading expectations? Here's the problem: if you have very unrealistic expectations, it's almost certain that you'll fail. It's because unrealistic expectations can't be met and therefore, there are zero chances for success.

One of the most unrealistic expectations surrounding day trading is being able to double one's initial trading capital in a couple of months, at most. Similar to such expectations is that of being able to quit one's day job and live an abundant life in just a few months via day trading. Successful day traders went through numerous failures, too, before they succeeded at day trading and were able to do it for a living.

If you decide to give day trading a shot, have realistic expectations. In fact, don't even expect to profit soon. Instead, take the initial losses as they come, limiting them through sensible stop-loss limits and learning from them. Eventually, you'll get the hang of it and your day trading profits will start eclipsing your day trading losses.

Changing Strategies Frequently

Do you know how to ride a bike? If not, do you know someone who does? Whether it's you or somebody you know, learning how to ride a bike wasn't instant. It took time and a couple of falls and bruises along the way.

But despite falls, scratches and bruises, you or that person you know stuck to learning how to ride a bike and with enough time and practice, succeeded in doing so. It was because you or the other person knew that initial failures mean that riding a bike was impossible. It's just challenging at first.

It's the same with learning how to day trade profitably. You'll need to give yourself enough time and practice to master it. Just because you suffered trading losses in the beginning doesn't mean it's not working or it's not for you. It probably means you haven't really mastered it yet.

But if you quit and shift to a new trading strategy or plan quickly, you'll have to start again from scratch, extend your learning time, and possibly lose more money than you would've if you stuck around to your initial strategy long enough to give yourself a shot at day trading successfully or concluding with certainty that it's not working for you.

If you frequently change your day trading strategies, i.e., you don't give yourself enough time to learn day trading strategies, your chances of mastering them become much lower. In that case, your chance of succeeding in day trading becomes much lower too.

Not Analyzing Past Trades

"Those who don't learn history are doomed to repeat it," said writer and philosopher George Santayana. We can paraphrase it to apply to day traders, too: "Those who don't learn from their day trading mistakes will be doomed to repeat them."

If you don't keep a day trading journal containing records of all your trades and more importantly, analyze them, you'll be doomed to repeat your losing day trades. It's because by not doing so, you won't be able to determine what you're doing wrong and what you should be doing instead in order to have more profitable day trades than losing ones.

As another saying goes: if you always do what you always did, you'll always get what you always got. Unless you analyze your past day trades on a regular basis, you'll be doomed to repeating the same mistakes and continue losing money on them.

Ditching Correlations

We can define correlations as a relationship where one thing influences the outcome or behavior of another. A positive correlation means that both tend to move in the same direction or exhibit similar behaviors, i.e., when one goes up, the other goes up, too, and vice versa.

Correlations abound in the stock market. For example, returns on the stock market are usually negatively correlated with the Federal Reserve's interest rates, i.e., when the Feds increase interest rates, returns on stock market investments go down and vice versa.

Correlations exist across industries in the stock market, too. For example, property development stocks are positively correlated to steel and cement manufacturing stocks. This is because when the property development's booming, it buys more steel and cement from manufacturing companies, which in turn also increase their income.

Ignoring correlations during day trading increase your risks for erroneous position taking and exiting. You may take a short position on a steel manufacturer's stock while taking a long position on a property development company's stock and if they have a positive correlation, one of those two positions will most likely end up in a loss.

But caution must be exercised with using correlations in your day trades. Don't establish correlations where there's none. Your job is to simply identify if there are observable correlations, what those correlations are, and how strong they are.

Being Greedy

Remember the story of the goose that lay golden eggs? Because the goose's owner was so greedy and couldn't wait for the goose to lay more eggs immediately, he killed the goose and cut it open.

Sadly, for the owner, there were no golden eggs inside the goose because it only created and laid one

When it comes to day trading, greed can have the same negative financial impact. Greed can make a day trader hold on to an already profitable position longer than needed and result in smaller profits or worse, trading losses.

That's why you must be disciplined enough to stick to your day trading stop-loss and profit-taking limits. And that's why you should program those limits on your platform, too. Doing so minimizes the risks of greed hijacking your otherwise profitable day trades.

CHAPTER 23:

Difference Between Swing Trading and Day Trading

I f you are a beginner, then keep your mind open for both types of trading, do not waste your money or time in investing until you do not have enough knowledge about the trading systems. For a beginner, there are always a lot of things to learn about; whatever the field is learning about your interest is very important. Before starting any trading pattern, it is necessary to understand your needs and expectations that you have related to the trading system. First of all, the trader who wants to trade should know how much active trading he wants. What are his current requirements and expectations related to trading whether he can handle his trading system for a long time, or did he have enough stamina to bear the loss? Once you decide the right path that suits you and that you believe can fulfill your expectation, and then you can easily survive in the trading market.

Traders have divided trading into two parts swing trading and day trading. This will help you to understand the difference between both the trading systems, and it will help you in choosing which trading system is best for you. The main goal of any beginner is to gain profit on their stock, whether it's a day trader or a swing trader; at the end of the day, every trader needs their name in a profit list even though both trading has different tools and technical analysis procedures.

Day trading is about making multiple trades in a day. As the name suggests doing trade on your stock within a day but multiple times is day trading. This trade is all about doing trade within a day or hours. You cannot go beyond that time, and it doesn't matter how many times you trade in a day. The main objective of the day traders is to make money from their preexisting income in a day with their stock. This trade is only about day trading; it does not contain night hours. They do not keep any overnight securities. The biggest advantage of day trading is that the trader has fewer chances of having any kind of loss. For example, if a trader invests their money on any stock and the market rate of that stock goes down in the middle of the night, so in that case, the trader has to face a loss, but because of day trading, the chances of losses are also less as they will not invest their money for overnight.

The day traders do not need any partner, they usually work alone, and they do not have their flexible schedule, and they do their work according to their mood and needs. They usually work at their places and take off and rap all of their stuff whenever they want. They do not need anyone's instruction because they do their work independently.

Sometimes it becomes difficult for the beginners of day traders to compete in the market because except making money and position in the market they also have to compete with the high-frequency traders, whereas other faces more advantages than the beginners as they become professionals in their work and have more experience than them. Once you start getting profit on your stock, there will be no come back from this earning adventure; you will desire to invest more and earn more.

The day trader has to generate a lot of effort and use his skills to maintain the position in the market. A beginner who wants to have all the luxuries firstly had to quit his job to maintain all his focus on trading because it would not be easy for a day trader to continue his job as it all depends on you to keep check and balance in the market. He should be aware of multiple screening so it will help him to spot the trading opportunities.

It can be done by having just one computer, and with conventional trading tools unlike, day trading it does not require the art technology. Swing traders have overnight leverage of 50% as compared to day trading, but this margin can be risky too, particularly if margin calls occur. These trading are not so much about what you want to trade, be it commodities, i.e., oil futures or stock from the CAC 40. Instead of that, it is simply all about timing. So, where it took 4 hours and daily charts of day trading, it will be more concerned about swing trading where it took multi-day charts and candlestick patterns. Moving average crossovers, Head and shoulders patterns, shooting stars, etc. are some of the most popular. It can be extremely challenging in two markets, the bear market environment or raging bull market. Here you will see even highly active traders will not display in the same position there will be same up and down oscillation. To invest in the stock market, it's compulsory to have a well-organized method for trading. It is very important to keep things simple, as in the early stages, it will look a bit difficult for the beginners, but instead of getting panic, they should handle them with confidence. This is another reason why this trade has a distinct advantage over other approaches to invest in a swing trade. Swing traders use technical analysis indicators to identify the price swings in the market and determine the condition of the market, whether a stock price will drop or rise in the short run. Through this, they invest capitalize in securities that have momentum and select the best time for buying or selling the stock. These technical analysis indicators help the traders to use the swing charts for their swing trading on the security current situation trend. To analyze the current trading pattern, swing traders use swing trading charts, which help the trader in providing data based on statistical analysis. Swing trading is not about the long term value of the security; instead of that, they are just concerned about the ups and downs in the stock price. Swing traders can make large returns on the stock that decay in value over time because they are making returns on each small price swing of their stock while the overall trend is downward. Swing trading and day trading appears similar in some aspects of trading. The main factor of trading is setting the two techniques apart and maintaining the position on time in the market. Unlike day traders, it does not close within minutes or in hours; it takes several weeks and overnight days. Swing traders can check their positions in the market periodically and can take action when critical points are reached.

Main differences between swing trading and day trading are:

Trading Times

Both of them have different timings of trading. In day trading, it takes a maximum of two to four hours daily for trading purposes, and in this time, the trader manages to analyze the charts, entering and getting out of the positions, and assessment different stocks. Whereas the swing trader's minimum needs 45 minutes in a day, update his order and find the new one. Day trading demands more time than swing trading.

Risks

Day trader experiences more losses than swing traders because day traders may need to carry out six trades per day, whereas swing traders may need to carry out six trades per month to maintain a good position in the market. That's why day traders had to face more struggle in maintaining their position in the market as their risk level is higher than swing traders, and they had to engage their selves more in the market then swing traders.

Stress

Day traders are more in stress as they have to keep their selves engage all the time with the market situation. They need great knowledge about market movements and had a great level of patience. A day trader needs to be more focused on their work. On the other hand, swing traders do not take that much pressure and can't say that they are much focused than day traders.

CHAPTER 24:

Risk and Account Management

rofessional informal investors utilize a hazard the executive strategy called the 1-percent hazard rule, or change it marginally to accommodate their exchanging strategies. Adherence to the standard downplays capital misfortunes when a dealer has an off day or encounters unforgiving economic situations, while as yet taking into account incredible month to month returns or salary. The 1-percent hazard principle bodes well for some reasons, and you can profit by comprehension and utilizing it as a feature of your exchanging system.

The 1-Percent Risk Rule

Following the standard methods, you never hazard more than 1 percent of your record an incentive on a solitary exchange. That doesn't imply that on the off chance that you have a $30,000 exchanging account, you can just purchase $300 worth of stock, which would be 1 percent of $30,000.

You can utilize the majority of your capital on a solitary exchange, or much more in the event that you use influence. Actualizing the 1-percent hazard principle implies you make chance administration strides with the goal that you counteract misfortunes of more than 1 percent on any single exchange.

Nobody wins each exchange, and the 1 percent hazard standard shields a broker's capital from declining fundamentally in horrible circumstances. In the event that you chance 1 percent of your present record balance on each exchange, you would need to lose 100 exchanges a line to crash your record. On the off chance that learner brokers pursued the 1-percent rule, a lot a greater amount of them would make it effectively through their first exchanging year.

Gambling 1 percent or less per exchange may appear to be a modest quantity to certain individuals, however, it can in any case give extraordinary returns. In the event that you hazard 1 percent, you should likewise set your benefit objective or desire on each effective exchange to 1.5 percent to 2 percent or more. When making a few exchanges every day, picking up a couple of rate focuses for you every day is totally conceivable, regardless of whether you just win half of your exchanges.

Applying the Rule

By gambling 1 percent of your record on a solitary exchange, you can make an exchange which gives you a 2-percent return for you, despite the fact that the market just moved a small amount of a percent. Also, you can chance 1 percent of your record regardless of whether the value normally moves 5 percent or 0.5 percent. You can accomplish this by utilizing targets and stop-misfortune orders.

You can utilize the standard to day exchange stocks or different markets, for example, prospects or forex. Expect you need to purchase a stock at $15, and you have a $30,000 account. You take a gander at the outline and see the value as of late put in a transient swing low at $14.90.

You put in a stop-misfortune request at $14.89, one penny beneath the ongoing low cost. When you have recognized your stop-misfortune area, you can figure what number of offers to purchase while taking a chance with close to 1 percent of your record.

Your record hazard likens to 1 percent of $30,000, or $300. Your exchange hazard approaches $0.11, determined as the distinction between your stock purchase cost and stop misfortune cost.

Separation your record hazard by your exchange hazard to get the best possible position size: $300/$0.11 = 2,727 offers. Round this down to 2,700 and this shows what number of offers you can purchase in this exchange without presenting yourself to misfortunes of more than 1 percent of your record. Note that 2,700 offers at $15 cost $40,500, which surpasses the estimation of your $30,000 record balance. Thusly, you need influence of in any event 2:1 to make this exchange.

On the off chance that the stock value hits your stop-misfortune, you will lose around 1 percent of your capital or near $300 for this situation. In any case, if the value moves higher and you sell your offers at $15.22, you make right around 2 percent on your cash, or near $600 (less commissions). This is on the grounds that your position is aligned to make or lose just about 1 percent at each $0.11

the cost moves. In the event that you exit at $15.33, you make very nearly 3 percent on the exchange, despite the fact that the value just moved around 2 percent.

This strategy enables you to adjust exchanges to a wide range of economic situations, regardless of whether unpredictable or quiet and still profit. The strategy likewise applies to all business sectors. Prior to exchanging, you ought to know about slippage where you can't get out at the stop misfortune cost and could assume a greater misfortune than anticipated.

Rate Variations

Merchants with exchanging records of under $100,000 ordinarily utilize the 1 percent standard. While 1 percent offers more security, when you're reliably gainful, a few merchants utilize a 2 percent hazard rule, gambling 2 percent of their record esteem per exchange. A center ground would be just gambling 1.5 percent or some other rate underneath 2 percent.

For records over $100,000, numerous merchants hazard under 1 percent. For instance, they may hazard as meager as 0.5 percent or even 0.1 percent on a huge record. While momentary exchanging, it winds up hard to hazard even 1 percent in light of the fact that the position sizes get so enormous. Every broker finds a rate they feel great with and that suits the liquidity of the market wherein they exchange. Whichever rate you pick, keep it beneath 2 percent.

Withstanding Losses

The 1-percent principle can be changed to suit every merchant's record size and market. Set a rate you feel great gambling, and afterward, compute your position size for each exchange as per the unit cost and stop misfortune.

Following the 1-percent guideline implies you can withstand a long series of misfortunes. Expecting you have bigger winning exchanges than failures then you locate your capital doesn't drop in all respects rapidly, however rise at a great rate. Before taking a chance with any cash—even 1 percent—practice your procedure in a demo record and work to make steady benefits before contributing your genuine capital.

Position Size

Not gambling an excessive amount of cash on some random exchange is fundamental for any informal investor. Tragically, when a great many people begin exchanging, they don't consider the hazard that they are taking – just about the potential prizes.

Each exchanging methodology must think about the most extreme level of the all-out exchanging capital that ought to be gambled in any one exchange. Truth be told, a broker's capacity to confine his misfortunes is similarly as significant (or much increasingly significant) as his accomplishment in overseeing winning positions.

Consider it. On the off chance that a merchant misfortune a modest quantity on each exchange, won't he remain in the game much more? Taking immense misfortunes is one of the essential reasons why such a large number of dealers don't make due around here. For what reason do brokers submit money related suicide along these lines, you may inquire? In the event that every single enormous misfortune begin little, shouldn't it be anything but difficult to keep a little misfortune from getting to be unmanageable? The appropriate response is a resonating "YES."

Restricting misfortunes in day exchanging includes a great deal of good judgment. In the first place, I don't figure any merchant should hazard more than 2 to 5% of his exchanging capital on some random exchange. Why? In the event that a dealer adheres to a 1% to 2% most extreme misfortune rule, his odds of remaining in the game are incredibly expanded in light of the fact that it will take numerous continuous misfortunes to clear him out and he will have more cash making openings accessible to him.

In the event that a merchant will deal with a $10,000 account, he ought not to lose more than $100 to $200 (1% to 2%) on each position taken. Utilizing a similar thinking, on the off chance that we are managing an exchanging account that is $100,000 in size, the most extreme suitable misfortune can be expanded to $1,000 or $2,000 per exchange. In light of these rates and on the sum the cost can move against the broker (decided from the graphs), he can compute the most extreme size his position ought to have. This turns out to be much clearer with a numerical model:

Position Sizing Example utilizing Currencies (to get familiar with monetary standards, read this segment)

Accept that a financial specialist can exchange a ton of one hundred thousand United States Dollars starting out with a nest of two thousand dollars (that's a fifty against one influence) and that the trader has ten thousand dollars in a record. With this record size, he can exchange a limit of five parcels (2000 dollars per five parcels in his edge store = ten thousand) at any given moment – however is this a savvy activity? We should investigate this somewhat further.

Hazard in day exchanging (or in some other type of hypothesis) must be controlled. One compelling method for overseeing danger is by not taking on a position bigger than a record of a given size can deal with. While a few creators and "specialists" have convoluted methods for deciding position size, these strategies will in general confound dealers and moderate them down. The one to two percent rule is easier to use as I would like to think. It is good judgment more than everything else. Try not to turn into another exchanging measurement by using stop orders as a defensive measurement; you can really mitigate your losses. Peruse further stop options by considering this tactic.

CHAPTER 25:

Order Types

Trading is somewhat more complex than just buying and selling. There are various ways you can buy and sell using different order types, and each order has its distinct function. With the growing awareness of the importance of the internet and digital technology, several investors now prefer to trade for themselves rather than pay large commissions to advisors to execute trades. But, before you can begin to buy and sell stocks, you need to know the different order types and when to use them.

Market Order

A market order, which is the most basic type of trade, is an order to buy or sell security instantly, irrespective of what the price is at the moment. This type of order gives assurance that the order will be applied but does not give assurance of the execution price. A market order generally will come to play at or near the present bid. So, if you want to buy a stock immediately, you will buy at a price that is close to or at the posted Ask. To sell a stock with this order type, you will be credited at a price that is close to or at the posted Bid.

However, traders need to know that market order may not be executed at the last traded price of that stock, especially in a volatile and fast moving market.

The only time the price remains the same is if the bid and ask prices are exactly the same as the last traded price. This order type is popularly used by traders who need to sell or purchase a stock without any delays.

One advantage of this order type is that you have the assurance that your trade order will be filled, in fact, it will be done ASAP. And even if you can't tell the particular price for the execution, market orders on securities that trade above tens of thousands of shares each day are likely to execute close to the ask and bid prices.

Limit order

This type of order is also referred to as pending orders. It allows traders to buy and sell securities or stocks at a defined or better price in the future. This order type executes a trade only if the price hits the pre-set price if not, the order remains open.

So, a limit order sets the minimum or maximum price you want to sell or buy a stock. For instance: An investor wants to buy shares of XYZ stock for not more than $20. The investor will fill a limit order for $20. In essence, the investor will not pay more than $20 for that stock, but he can buy the stock for less than $20.

193

We have four types of limit orders. Let us look at each below:

- **Sell Limit**

This is an order type set to sell a security or stock above or exactly at a specified price. To get the best price, you need to place the order above or at the current market ask.

- **Buy Limit**

This is an order to buy a stock below or exactly at a specified price. To get the best price, you need to place the order below or at the current market bid.

- **Sell Stop**

This is an instruction to sell a stock at a price that is below the current market asked. This order type only gets filled once the trade gets to the pre-determined price level. Sell stop orders are placed below the market while the buy stops are placed above the market. Once a trade hits the stop level, it instantly converts into a limit order or market order. This type of order is used to exit long trades.

- **Buy Stop Order**

This is an instruction to purchase a stock at a price that is above the current market bid. Just like the sell stop, this order type only gets filled once the trade gets to the pre-determined price level. This order type is used as a stop-loss on short positions, particularly when the price is moving against you.

Stop-Loss Order

This is also known as an on-stop buy, on-stop sell, or stopped market. This order type is one of the most useful orders and differs from market order and limit orders. For this order type, the order stays dormant until it passes a certain price, then it gets activated as a market order. For example, if you place a stop-loss sell order on ABC shares at $50 per share, the order will remain dormant until the price gets to or goes below $50. It will then convert into a market order and then sell the shares at the best price in the market. This type of order is used for traders who do not have the luxury of time to monitor the market continually but want to protect them from massive downside move. The best time to apply this type of order is before you go on a vacation or long trips.

Stop-Limit Order

This order type is similar to the stop-loss orders, but for this type of order, there is a set limit on the price at which they should execute. The stop-limit order has two specified prices: the limit price and the stop price (the stop price converts the order to a sell order). Instead of the order to convert to a market order to sell, the sell order converts to a limit order, which will only execute when it hits the limit price or a better price.

All or None (AON)

This is popularly used by traders who purchase penny stocks. The order ensures that you get your complete order quantity or nothing at all. This becomes a problem if a limit is placed on the order or if the requested stock is not liquid. For instance, you place an order to purchase 1,000 shares of ABC, but the company is only selling 500 shares at the time. This type of order means that your request will not be filled until the available shares are up to 1o00 and available at your set price. But if you did not place an all-or-none order, your order for 1,000 shares will partially be filled with 500 shares.

Fill or Kill (FOK)

This order type is a combination of the AON and the IOC (Immediate or cancel). This order commands that the whole order size be traded within a limited time, usually within seconds. The order gets canceled if the condition is not met.

Immediate or Cancel (IOC)

This order commands that only the amount of an order that can be executed within a very short time, usually a few seconds should be filled while the remaining of the order should be canceled. If none of the shares is traded within the given interval, the trade gets canceled totally.

Take Profit

This type of order is sometimes referred to as a profit target. The aim is to close out a trade at a profit after it has gotten to a specified level. Once the Take profit order is executed, the trade position closes. This order type is always linked to an open position of a pending order.

Good till Cancelled (GTC)

This type of order places time restrictions on different orders. The orders stay active until you move to cancel them. For most brokerages, the maximum time you can leave an order active is 90 days.

Day

This order type is a follow up on the GTC, in the sense that, if you did not place an expiry date on the GTC instruction, the order automatically gets set to one-day order. So, once the trading day is over, that particular order expires. You would have to re-enter the trade the following day if it did not get filled the earlier day.

Level 2 Trading

Level 2 is a subscription-based service that gives traders real-time access to the NASDAQ order book. In this NASDAQ order book, you will find price quotes for every price level, the size on each order as well as which market maker has what order. On the left side of the Level 2 window, you will find the bid prices and sizes while the right side shows the ask prices and sizes.

This service arms traders with detailed price information, including available prices as posted by electronic communication networks, and market makers. Electronic Communication Networks are computerized orders, and anyone can trade using the ECNs, even the big traders use this ECN. Market makers give the market its liquidity; however, they can mess with traders' stop losses. Market makers are obligated to buy and sell when no one else is doing so. Therefore, they determine the market in a way.

One thing you need to understand, though, is that not every order that disappears from the level 2 window is executed. Level 2 is an order book and so contains all the live orders in the market. Sellers and buyers can decide to pull out their orders at any time, which is why you will see orders disappear.

Level 2 order book is very important, particularly for active traders that want to know where the interest of buyers and sellers is in the market.

While level 1 provides traders with needed information like best bid and ask prices, the level 2 goes further to display the supply and demand of the price levels outside the NBBO (National Best Bid Offer) price. The user gets to see visual display of price ranges and connected liquidity at each price level. Traders then use this information to determine entry and exit points that offer enough liquidity that a trader needs to complete the trade.

Benefits of the Level 2 Service

One major benefit of this service is that it offers access to rich information that concerns the market. A trader can maximize this information in several ways to make a profit. For instance, the window helps a trader to know the order sizes and liquidity volumes for stocks traded on NASDAQ. You can also identify trends by using data from the bid and ask orders.

The level 2 quotes also provide important data related to institutional investors and market makers that a trader can use to maximize his profit. For instance, you can know an institutional trader's interest in a large stock by looking at their order sizes, and then you place your identical orders. You can use this same strategy with reserve orders (these are large orders that are broken into smaller sizes.) After you have discovered hidden orders by looking at the Level 2 window, you can then place your identical order because when institutional traders invest in a stock, they help the resistance and support levels for the price of that stock.

CHAPTER 26:

How to Start Forex Trading

orex trading is not a trade that one can pull off without breaking a sweat before exchanging currencies. There has to be prior preparation, studies done and analysis of the market patterns to make the first trade.

There are a lot of terms used that are new to a trader who is just starting off and are vocabularies to them. It would do well to an aspiring trader to acquaint themselves with the new terms and understand the meaning behind them and how to use them appropriately when trading. This will prove essential to avoid miscomprehension of certain concepts when trading. To new traders, the terms may be a little bit difficult and also have a completely different meaning than the expected one from its word-formation. The following words below are some of the new vocabularies that will be encountered by a new trader, which are common in the language of trading.

A Pip

A pip is the lowest measure of the value of movement of currency under observation. The term pip is, however, an abbreviation of the term-percentage in point. A pip, as the lowest measurable value of the movement that the currency makes, always measures ad 1% of the currency that a trader wants to exchange. When in the forex market a currency increases or decreases by a single pip, the inference has the meaning that the currency either increased or decreased by 1%. A great example is when the market analysis tools show that the US dollar has increased by a pip. This is to mean that the US dollar has increased in its value by $0.0001.

That is how a pip is inferred and its meaning. Trade is always made in terms of pips, and a trader can make trades with many pips as possible. This is because the pips are the lowest value that is measured by the currency.

Base Currency

The base currency is the type of currency that a trader has and is currently holding. The base currency is likely the currency of the country that you're from. If a trader is from the US, his or her base currency will be the US dollar. If the trader is from the UK, the base currency of the trader will be the pound. The base currencies of traders are different across many traders around the globe due to different geographical differences.

Asking Price

The asking price is a term that is used to refer to the amount of money that your broker firm will demand from or will ask from you when you are making a trade. A broker always demands this price or this amount of money when they are accepting the pair of currencies to be traded from you. The price id for buying the quote that you've made of the pair of currencies. A note to be made is that the asking price; made by the brokerage firms, is always higher than the bid price.

Bid Price

The bid price is mostly used in reference to the brokerage firms, where it is the amount of money that the brokers will be willing to buy or to bid the base currency that you are currently holding. The broker firm sets the bid price according to their ability to bid on the base currency that has.

Quote Currency

The quote currency, unlike the base currency, is the currency that a trader wants and is willing to purchase, in exchange for his or her base currency. If a trader wants to exchange US dollars to get South African Rand, the currency of South Africa; the Rand is the quote currency. It is always stroked against the base currency when trading and when the currencies are made into pairs.

The Spread

This is the commission that the broker firm receives from being a platform where forex trading can take place. When referred to, the spread means the difference in value between the bid price made by the broker and the asking price, also quoted by the broker.

Finding the Right Broker Firm

So as to trade forex, you will have to have a brokerage firm that will be an online platform from which you'll open and close trade. Finding the right broker firm is an important process for other brokers can be a sham out to cheat people of their money. It is, therefore, paramount that a trader carries out research on the available broker firms and picks out the best and one that is highly recommended for its services. When deciding on which broker firm to go with look and ask the bid price that the broker quotes and other important aspects, including the margin and the leverage level that they offer. The customer service should also be top-notch for the broker, which will be great for a trader who is just starting off. Most of the broker companies also offer studies on how to carry out forex trading and those come in handy to the new traders.

Making an Analysis of the Worldwide Economy

To make gains and profits and gains in trades that you are going to make, analyzing the economic trends of the worldwide economy is of great import to be fully aware of the factors that may trigger the currencies to increase or decrease in value. This is important in making a correct prediction on the pair of currencies you're exchanging, whether they will make a profit or a loss. Factors that are important to look into when evaluating the global economy are like the political climate of countries whose currencies have a strong value, natural factors that may influence the economy of countries, the Gross Domestic Product of the country whose currency you want to exchange with your base currency, and other minor factors such as the investment rate of the said country.

Evaluating which countries are looking up to growth and development opportunities are also important in determining the quote currency to use impairing up currencies to make a trade. Also on the analysis of the worldwide economy, when the currency of the country you seek to purchase in exchange of your base currency is doing well and is set to increase in its value, convert your base currency into the quote currency. On the other hand, convert the quote currency into the base currency in case its value increases.

There are various online sites that have analysis tools on the economic performance of different countries that you may seek for them to be your quote currency. Others rank counties in terms of their GDP that makes it easier for you to choose the countries that are projected for growth and development. Being in touch with the trending news globally is a plus in getting information relevant to trading forex.

A new forex trader may subscribe to a few forex trading channels and outlets to be constantly on toes of events and happenings that may trigger the value of currencies to either increase or decrease, which may result in the reversal of the outlook of the trade made. Having relevant information at all times is key in making gains and preventing the loss of your money and probably your account is cleared.

Opening the First Trade

Pairing currencies and making the first trade; opening and closing a trade happens when the quote currency is to be paired by the base currency have been paired and there is an opportune trading window. Opening a trade is making an order to purchase a certain currency and in exchange for your base current through your broker firm. You'll have the analysis tools that are commonly offered by the brokers in software programs.

The execution of making an order in some platforms might be instant while in some other platforms, it might be a tad bit slower. Nonetheless, most brokerage firms offer live prices and values of the currencies that are too traded and their exchange rates and the instant changes to their values are displayed. The first trade for a new trader might just be one or others might open up new trades over a short period of time. It is advisable that just several enough trades be opened, which the new trader is comfortable and at ease in trading.

CHAPTER 27:

7 Rules of Day Trading

Day Trading is the ability to buy and sell financial instruments within the same trading day. There is a group of day traders called the pattern day traders (PDT) these are just traders who make more than four trades within five days and who use a margin account to trade. Day Trading has rules, and failure to adhere to certain rules can be costly. Rules also vary depending on location and the volume you trade.

The following rules of Day Trading, if used correctly, can help traders make profits and avoid huge losses.

How to Enter and Exit a Market

Day traders should have a predetermined plan in place of when to enter and exit a market. A trader can quickly find yourself out of the game as soon as you press the enter key if they do not have a plan. As a day trader, you have to accept the fact that you do not control the market. Therefore, one of the key factors to succeeding in Day Trading is usually determined by your ability to enter and exit your trading positions. Knowing the prices at which you wish to enter and exit can help make profits or save you from losing out on more.

When making the plan:

- Use indicators
- Set a target price before you enter the market.
- Know how much stock you plan to trade
- Plan for when to exit the market — when the market is going against your expectations, do you exit your position to avoid bigger losses?

Trading Rush Hours

Another important Day Trading rule is to avoid the first hour after the market opens and the last hour before it closes. It is wise to wait and observe during those times. Do not be eager to jump in as soon as the market opens. The first and last hours are the most volatile times in the market. This is because the stock is likely reacting to some overnight news releases, and this is when the big investors and trading experts compete. In the last hour, traders are also rushing to close out their positions.

Be Cautious of Margin Trading

Another important rule is to trade with the money you have, not borrowed money. It is important to be cautious of margin trading as it increases your purchasing power and allows you to use borrowed money to increase financial leverage; however, not all trades are profitable. Therefore, you risk losing the small bit of your capital as well as the borrowed money. Margin trading should be used in trades that you are sure will be profitable.

Be Realistic

Another important Day Trading rule is to avoid greed. It is very easy to be carried away by greed when trading, do not lose out on small profits because you think you can make more. It is very important to remain realistic about profits. The market is always changing; sometimes, it is better to settle on a small profit than to make big losses.

Be Knowledgeable

Do not day trade if you do have no sufficient knowledge of what is happening in the markets. Not everyone can trade in the market. Most traders start with paper trading and intense training. You need to be aware of information about the stocks you plan to trade, basic trading procedures, and always be on the lookout for anything that can affect your stocks. You can start by practicing using a demo account; this is a trial and error account, where you do not use real money. This account enables traders to experiment with trading before they can set up a real funded account.

Cut Your Losses

This is the number one rule in trading; cut your losses. Placing a trade is taking a risk; every trader, even the best in the world, has had bad trading days. Losing is part of trading. Traders need to accept their losses when the market starts going against them instead of hoping for a turnaround. This can be a lethal mistake. Have an exit strategy and react accordingly. Accepting your loss reduces the chance of it happening again. By cutting your losses, you learn from it and make the necessary changes to avoid a repetition.

Risk Management Plan

Risk management plans help cut down losses. The idea is to avoid risking more than you can afford to lose. With a risk management plan, even when a trade goes wrong, they still have money to trade tomorrow. Traders follow the 1% rule, which allows them to trade only 1% of their capital on any single trade. This ensures that only 1% of their money is at risk on any single trade.

CHAPTER 28:

Trading Psychology

To succeed in day trading, day traders require many skills, including the ability to analyze a technical chart. But none of the technical skills can replace the importance of a traders' mind-set. Discipline, quick thinking, and emotional control; all these are collectively called the trading psychology and are important factors for succeeding in the day trading business.

On the surface, day trading is an easy activity; markets go up and down and traders buy and sell with the price. Then how come 90% of traders make losses in day trading? The answer lies in trading psychology where most of the day traders fail. You will see many online courses advertising to teach day trading or technical analysis, but It is unheard of any course that teaching trading psychology to traders.

It is a well-known fact that controlling emotions of fear and greed are two of the most difficult decisions a day trader can take. Even those who prepare a trading plan, create trading rules; find it hard to stick to those rules and plans while trading in the stock markets. It is like dieting. When you are not supposed to think of ice cream, all you can do is think of ice cream.

Trading psychology identifies traders' mental and emotional state, which contributes to their success or failure in stock trading or trading any other financial security. Trading psychology is more important in day trading because here, traders must decide quickly and get to trade only for a few hours. It is like being boxed a small timeframe. For example, if a person is given two things to choose from, and given a time limit of 3 hours, he will do it in a relaxed way. However, if he is asked to decide within 3 seconds, he will panic. In other words, he will get into an emotional state.

Trading psychology involves two aspects; risk-taking and self-discipline. Traders know that emotions like greed and fear should not influence them, but they allow these emotions to affect their trading.

In greed, traders take more risk than is safe for them. Traders may try to place big trades in a hurry to earn profits. If their trades are profitable, they may refuse to exit these trades even if the exit point has come and continue holding positions hoping for bigger profits. This behavior ultimately ends with loss because markets do not keep trending in one direction. Eventually, the market trend changes and the profitable position turn into a loss-making one.

Fear has the opposite effect but the same result for traders. In the grip of fear, traders may close their position prematurely, and then trade again to earn profits. It becomes a vicious cycle of fear and greed, where the trader is afraid to keep the position open longer but keeps trading again in greed. This results in over trading and losses.

Fear and Day Trading

The technical progress has made it possible for news to travel quickly and reach far-flung places. This has created a unique situation for stock markets, where the positive news has a quick and positive reaction in the stock markets; but negative news causes sudden and a steep drop in stock prices as traders become gripped by fear and panic.

In situations leading to greed, traders still pause and think, if they are being greedy. But under the influence of fear, traders usually overreact and exit their position quickly. This has a chain-reaction effect on markets. Prices fall, traders sell in fear; prices fall further, traders sell more in fear. This emotion creates bigger ripples in stock markets than greed. Traders exit from their positions fearing that they will lose their profits or make losses. The fear of loss paralyzes novice traders when their positions turn into loss-making. They refuse to exit such positions, hoping for a bounce-back in markets, hoping to turn their losses into profits. What should have been a small loss, eventually turns into a big one for them, sometimes even wiping out their all trading capital. A rationally thinking person will quickly exit from such a position. But fear is such strong emotion in day trading, that it stops even rational people from taking correct decisions.

Rule-Based Trading

To protect yourself from psychological risks in day trading, you must take steps to eliminate this before you start trading. There is only one thing that can protect you from the emotional rollercoaster ride in stock markets, which is a ruled based trading system.

All aspects of your day trading must be governed by a set of rules, which will involve your trading plan and trading strategies. Every day, you must go over these rules and trade accordingly.

Before you trade, sit down and think, why will you start day trading? Are you going to do it for a side income? Are you going to do it for the excitement of stock markets? Or, are you going to do it to prove any point to somebody? Many traders fall into the egotistical trap of proving themselves right in trading. They will keep trading against the market and expect the market to change its course, instead of changing their trading style.

If you are starting day trading to earn a living, then this thought should always be uppermost in your mind. You cannot allow yourself to be distracted by small profits and losses and trade indiscriminately. This should be your goal, to earn a living, and it should be your aim of day trading every day. Before you trade, remind yourself that you are doing this for a living, not for the short-term excitement. Therefore, if you make any loss, remind yourself that in business, difficulties are a part of the cycle. Try to maintain a neutral mental state whether you make profits and losses. All your trades must be done according to your plans and strategy. Before you take any trade, know the risk-reward ratio; why you enter that trade; and when you will exit the trade with a profit or at a stop loss.

Create rules about:

- How many trades you will make every day?

- What will be your loss tolerance limit for a single session?

- What will be your profit target for one session?

Stop trading when any of these three criteria are completed. For example, if you decided to take only two trades in a session, stop trading for that session once you have completed your two trades, whether your trades were profitable. If you have created a threshold of $20 loss for a single station, stop trading if you have reached that loss limit for the session. This will teach you disciplined trading, and you will consciously try to keep your losses to a minimum.

A similar rule should be applied for profit booking. Stop trading for the day if you have reached the profit target. This profit target could be in terms of a fixed amount, or the number of successful trades. For example, some traders stop trading once they have made a profitable trade. This is one of the best greed management techniques. If you have made a profit in stock trading, even if it is tiny, just pocket it and run away from markets. Otherwise, greed will take over and you will over-trade, trying to make more profit, and end up with losses.

Why Trading Psychology is Important

Most of the people fail in day trading because they start at the wrong end. They start by learning trading skills first, and then move on to money and risk management techniques, and the last stop is to learn, superficially, about trading psychology.

In fact, the right sequence of learning day trading should be learning the trading psychology first, and then money and risk management techniques and the last part should constitute learning the trading skills. It is very easy to learn technical analysis and how to use technical indicators. But it is very difficult to control one's emotions like fear and greed while trading, or astutely manage money while day trading.

If you look at people in different fields, you will find the mind-set is the main difference between those who reach the pinnacle of their chosen career and those who remain mediocre. Be it business, science, technology, sports, or any other creative pursuit, people who train their minds for success are the ones who win the race. In intraday trading also, hundreds and thousands of day traders use the same methods of technical analysis, however, only a few of them succeed in making profitable trade and others go home with losses. It is the trading psychology that makes the difference between successful traders and those who failed.

Every trader, who tries to learn day trading, knows that there are certain rules to be followed and still the majority of them fail to do so find; therefore, if you want to succeed in day trading, you must pay attention to how you react to markets. Stock trading is nothing but watching the price rise and fall and trading off with the trend. But still, traders fail to follow this simple method of trading. Day trading happens 90% in the mind of a day trader, and only 10% in what happens in markets. A day trader takes a decision based on what he or she thinks is going to happen in stock markets, and not on what is happening. This is the biggest mistake of day traders do and the reason is their emotions.

To overcome this psychological hurdle, day traders must learn how to manage their trades without emotions. They can do so only with the help of technology and self-discipline. If they do not have self-control or do not follow a disciplined trading plan, they cannot make profits in stock markets.

CHAPTER 29:

Tips for Market Investing

Maximizing Your Investments

There are several ways that investors may maximize their investments. Of course, practicing proper trading techniques will help investors to earn greater returns on their investments. However, there are several other ways in which investors may maximize their investments and improve the returns on those investments. They may decrease investment costs, increase diversification, rebalance, and practice other techniques to improve their investments. It is important to learn about all the possible ways to maximize one's investments because you don't know what you don't know. Every bit counts. Just saving a bit here and there will quickly add up and maximize the investments.

Investors may maximize their investments by decreasing the cost of investing. There are several ways that investing may cost money, and that money is coming directly out of the investment. Investors may switch from hiring a financial advisor to doing the investing themselves, cutting the costs of commission. Investors commonly forget about transaction costs. There is typically a flat fee for buying stock through a broker. Instead of making many small purchases, investors may save up and only buy stocks in certain increments (for example, perhaps the investor won't buy more stocks until they have saved $1000). By doing this, a much smaller percentage of the investment is being cut out and used to cover those fees. This may require more patience, but that money will add up. Lowering one's expenses will increase their return. Instead of being spent, that money may be growing and earning a return on it. Because of compound interest, this money will earn money on itself and multiply over a period of years. This is why it's crucial to save every bit possible.

Investors must also really pay attention to their portfolios. Diversification is crucial, and it can save the investor from losing all of their investment. Markets typically fall much more quickly than markets rise. This means that the investor must prepare for such occurrences. It is important to regularly rebalance one's portfolio to ensure that it is positioned correctly for the investor to make the largest possible gains.

Investors must also truly pay attention to what they want. Maximizing one's investments will depend on the person and what their goals are. Although it is wise to listen to the advice of experts and see what other ways that one may invest, it is crucial to follow the path that is best for the goals and preferences of the individual. This is why a plan is necessary and should be followed. Investors must not stop investing. This is another way to take advantage of compound interest. The investor's portfolio should never stop growing. This growth should be due to both growths in the investment and regular contributions by the investor themselves. Despite the great returns that may be experienced in a bull market, contributions are still necessary. Bear markets should also not discourage investors from continuing to invest; this can be a great time to get a good deal on a stock!

Retirement Plans

There are several savings plans that investors can get involved with. These can help to provide the investor with additional benefits that wouldn't be available to them otherwise.

One of these plans is a 401(k). This is a retirement savings plan that will be sponsored by an employer. This will allow the individual to invest their money before taxes so that they can save and invest some of their paychecks. The investor is not required to pay taxes until they withdraw this money from their account. Investors may control how to invest their money. It is common to have mutual funds that contain stocks, bonds, and money market investments.

However, there are also target-date funds, which are stocks and bonds that will decrease in risk as the investor nears their retirement age. Unlike individual investing, however, this plan may not offer its users complete freedom. For instance, most employees must work for a company for a certain period of time before gaining access to their payments.

Employees may even have to work for the company for a certain period of time before being able to enroll in a 401(k) at all. There are typical costs for withdrawing from these accounts before hitting retirement age as well. There are also contribution limits for each year. Investing for oneself, however, offers more freedom, and there are no limits on investing. For those working for an employer, however, this may be a good solution to investing using the paycheck given. It is a way to utilize the ability not to be taxed on one's investments from their paycheck. Employees may also enroll in Roth 401(k)s, which are not taxed for withdrawals. The better choice will depend on both the employee and the employer, as the plans are taxed differently.

403(b) plans are similar to 401(k)s, yet there are some slight differences. Both offer matching of the investments. For instance, for every dollar the employee contributes, the employer may contribute $0.50. This can prove to be greatly helpful to investors. The major difference between these are the employees that may enroll in these plans. Those in public schools, government jobs, nonprofits, and more may register for this plan. They are not for private-sector workers. Besides this, the plans are identical in their purposes. A 403(b) plan, however, may allow for faster vesting of funds and additional contributions, although the investment options may be less plentiful.

Direct Stock Purchase Plans

Direct stock purchase plans allow investors to directly purchase stock from the company without the use of a broker. These plans may be available directly to retail investors, yet some companies will use third-party administrators to handle the transactions. They will typically have lower fees and the potential for buying shares at a discounted price. This may not be an option for all companies. These plans may also come with restrictions on when the investor may purchase shares. This plan may appeal to long-term investors that lack the money for an initial investment otherwise.

The investor may choose to sign up once for this plan or they may sign up to make automatic and periodic investments through a transfer agent. This agent will maintain balances and record transactions. To keep costs low, transfer agents will typically carry out bulk transactions for the company each time period that they choose. Direct stock purchase plans are an alternative to using online brokerages, and they will typically cost less. Instead of paying higher transaction fees, the investor may pay a small purchase processing fee for each share that they purchase. These are usually quite a bit smaller than the transaction fees that investors must pay a brokerage. This means that the investor will have more money that they will be able to invest in. Instead of that money going to the brokerage, that money may be invested and generate a return for the investor. This can prove to be a wise move, especially for those wishing to buy a lesser amount of stocks. For those with greater funds for trading stocks, an online brokerage may prove more beneficial for the individual.

Direct stock purchase plans aren't for everyone. They will typically require investors to make a certain monthly commitment (i.e., $100) to investing. On the other hand, investors may buy stocks from a brokerage one time and never buy it again. Investors will also have to pay the market price for their stocks instead of being able to time it themselves. It may also be less convenient to create another account.

However, once started, this will be an automatic investment and won't cost as much as it would purchase stocks through a broker.

This plan works by the investor making monthly deposits and those deposits being put towards purchasing shares of the company's stock. New shares (or portions of shares) will be purchased each month based on the amount of money available from deposits and dividends. This is a simple way to acquire shares of a company's stock slowly. This is also inexpensive, as these plans typically have either low costs or no costs at all. They also have low minimum deposits, usually ranging from about $100 to $500, although this may vary. This is a great plan for those who lack the financial power to invest otherwise. A common way that these purchase plans are carried out is by combining them with dividend reinvestment plans. These may be combined with the direct stock purchase plans to maximize the amount that the investor is investing in.

Dividend Reinvestment Plans

Dividend reinvestment plans allow investors to, as the name suggests, reinvest their dividends. These are typically free to sign up for and quite easy to get started in. Investors must simply check a box or click a few buttons to sign up, and the dividends that they earn will go towards reinvesting into shares of stocks. Perhaps the investor gets a dividend for stock x. If they have signed up for DRIP (Dividend Reinvestment Plan), that dividend will go towards shares (or portions of shares) of purchasing more of stock x. This is a great way to manage one's investments automatically. On the dividend payment date, the investor's dividend will go towards reinvesting in that stock.

There are ways to sign up for this through the brokerage that one trades through or through an investment company. Instead of taking out these dividends and spending them, they may be used for greater benefits to the investor. This money can help the investor to make more money. Instead of being received as a check or deposited into the investor's bank, this money may be redeposited into more stocks for the investor. The investor should keep in mind, however, that these shares will be bought at market price and will typically be bought directly from the company, which is why this is free of transaction costs. These shares will also not be marketable through stock exchanges; they must be redeemed through the company directly.

There may be some limitations to this. Although these may be commission-free for the investor and may even have discounted share prices, DRIPs may have minimum dollar amounts that must be invested. There may be a minimum purchase amount for this. This is a great way for investors to take advantage of compound interest, as they are adding the extra amount that they may not have invested otherwise. However, the dividends may still be taxable, and the shares will be illiquid. The investor, once they have signed up, will not be able to regulate how much is and is not reinvested from these dividends. It is also a great way for investors to increase the number of shares of stock that they own without paying a commission for these shares. This is a more cost-effective approach than buying stock traditionally.

CHAPTER 30:

Understanding Diversification

What Is Diversification?

The term diversification in the world of finance refers to a growth strategy. This strategy makes full use of available opportunities in the market and allocating investment risk across various asset classes.

It is accurate to say that diversification is also a risk management approach to investing. Diversification makes use of a large variety of options in an investment portfolio. The reasoning that supports this approach claims that a portfolio that consists of different asset classes will basically result in higher returns while lowering risks associated with a single asset class.

Diversification focuses on asset allocation. It consists of a plan that endeavors to allocate funds or assets appropriately across a variety of investments. When an investor diversifies his or her portfolio, then there is some level of risk that has to be accepted. However, it is also advisable to devise an exit strategy so that the investor is able to let go of the asset and recoup their funds. This becomes necessary when a specific asset class is not yielding any worthwhile returns compared to others.

If an investor is able to create an aptly diversified portfolio, their investment will be adequately covered. An adequately diversified portfolio also allows room for growth. Appropriate asset allocation is highly recommended as it allows investors a chance to leverage risk and manage any possible portfolio volatility because different assets have varying reactions to adverse market conditions.

Investor Opinions on Diversifications

Different investors have varying opinions regarding the type of investment scenarios they consider to be ideal. Numerous investors believe that a properly diversified portfolio will likely bring in a double-digit return despite prevailing market conditions. They also agree that in the worst case situation will be simply a general decrease in the value of the different assets. Yet with all this information out there, very few investors are actually able to achieve portfolio diversification.

So why are investors unable to simply diversify their portfolios appropriately? The answers are varied and diverse. The challenges encountered by investors in diversification include weighting imbalance, hidden correlation, underlying devaluation, and false returns among others. While these challenges sound rather technical, they can easily be solved. The solution is also rather simple. By hacking these challenges, an investor will then be able to benefit from an aptly diversified platform.

The Process of Asset Class Allocation

There are different ways of allocating investments to assets. According to studies, most investors, including professional investors, portfolio managers, and seasoned traders actually rarely beat the indexes within their preferred asset class. It is also important to note that there is a visible correlation between the performance of an underlying asset class and the returns that an investor receives. In general, professional investors tend to perform more or less the same as an index within the same class asset.

Investment returns from a diversified portfolio can generally be expected to imitate the related asset class closely. Therefore, asset class choice is considered an extremely crucial aspect of an investment. In fact, it is the single more crucial aspect for the success of a particular asset class. Other factors such as individual asset selection and market timing only contribute about 6% of the variance in investment outcomes.

Wide Diversifications between Various Asset Classes

Diversification to numerous investors simply implies spreading their funds through a wide variety of stocks in different sectors such as health care, financial, energy, as well as medium caps, small, and large-cap companies. This is the opinion of your average investor. However, a closer look at this approach reveals that investors are simply putting their money in different sectors of stocks class. These asset classes can very easily fall and rise when the markets do.

A reliably diversified portfolio is one where the investor or even the manager is watchful and alert because of the hidden correlation that exists between different asset classes. This correlation can easily change with time and there are several reasons for this. One reason is international markets. Many investors often choose to diversify their portfolios with international stocks. However, there is also a noticeable correlation across the different global financial markets. This correlation is clearly visible not just across European markets but also emerging markets from around the world. There is also a clear correlation between equities and fixed income markets which are generally the hallmarks of diversification.

This correlation is actually a challenge and is probably a result of the relationship between structured financing and investment banking. Another factor that contributes to this correlation is the rapid growth and popularity of hedge funds. Take the case where a large international organization such as a hedge fund suffers losses in a particular asset class.

Should this happen, then the firm may have to dispose of some assets across the different asset classes. This will have a multiplier effect as numerous other investments and other investors will, therefore, be affected even though they had diversified their portfolios appropriately. This is a challenge that affects numerous investors who are probably unaware of its existence. They are also probably unaware of how it should be rectified or avoided.

Realignment of Asset Classes

One of the best approaches to solving the correlation challenge is to focus on class realignment. Basically, asset allocation should not be considered as a static process. Asset class imbalance is a phenomenon that occurs when the securities markets develop and different asset classes exhibit varied performance.

After a while, investors should assess their investments then diversify out of underperforming assets and instead shift this investment to other asset classes that are performing well and are profitable in the long term. Even then, it is advisable to be vigilant so that no one single asset class is over-weighted as other standard risks are still inherent. Also, a prolonged bullish market can result in overweighting one of the different asset classes which could be ready for a correction. Following are a couple of approaches that an investor can focus on.

Diversification and the Relative Value

Investors sometimes find asset returns to be misleading including veteran investors. As such, it is advisable to interpret asset returns in relation to the specific asset class performance. The interpretation should also take into consideration the risks that this asset class is exposed to and even the underlying currency.

When diversifying investments, it is important to think about diversifying into asset classes that come with different risk profiles. These should also be held in a variety of currencies. You should not expect to enjoy the same outcomes when investing in government bonds and technology stocks. However, it is recommended to endeavor to understand how each suits the larger investment objective.

By using such an approach, it will be possible to benefit more from a small gain from an asset within a market where the currency is increasing in value. This is as compared to a large gain from an asset within a market where the currency is in decline. As such, huge gains can translate into losses when the gains are reverted back to the stronger currency. This is the reason why it is advisable to ensure that proper research and evaluation of different asset classes are conducted.

Currency Considerations

Currency considerations are crucial when selecting asset classes to diversify in. take the Swiss franc for instance. It is one of the world's most stable currencies and has been that way since the 1940s. Because of this reason, this particular currency can be safely and reliably used to measure the performance of other currencies.

However, private investors sometimes take too long choosing and trading stocks. Such activities are both overwhelming and time-consuming. This is why, in such instances, it is advisable to approach this differently and focus more on the asset class. With this kind of approach, it is possible to be even more profitable. Proper asset allocation is crucial to successful investing. It enables investors to mitigate any investment risks as well as portfolio volatility. The reason is that different asset classes have different reactions to all the different market conditions.

Constructing a well-thought out and aptly diversified portfolio, it is possible to have a stable and profitable portfolio that even outperforms the index of assets. Investors also have the opportunity to leverage against any potential risks because of different reactions by the different market conditions.

Example:

An investor has a total of $100,000 to invest. The best approach is to put the funds in a diversified portfolio but the challenge is properly or adequately balancing the portfolio. The first step is to check out market conditions and then conduct an assessment of possible returns versus any likely risks. As such, the investor can choose to invest in very secure investments that are likely to produce long-term income.

Such an investment can include between 10 and 12 stocks that are highly diversified. These are generally stocks from different sectors, industries, and countries. This kind of diversification helps to leverage against any possible risks and also ensures the portfolio is thoroughly mixed.

CHAPTER 31:

Options Day Trading Rules for Success

There is more to options day trading to just having a style or a strategy. If that was all it took, then you could just adopt those that are proven to work and just stick with them. Yes, options day trading styles and strategy are important but they are not the end-all-be-all of this career.

The winning factor is the options day trader himself or herself. You are the factor that determines whether or not you will win or lose in this career. Only taking the time to develop your expertise, seeking guidance when necessary and being totally dedicated allows a person to move from a novice options day trader to an experienced one that is successful and hitting his or her target goals.

To develop into the options day trader you want to be, being disciplined is necessary. There are options day trading rules that can help you develop that necessary discipline. You will make mistakes. Every beginner in any niche does and even experienced options day traders are human and thus, have bad days too.

Knowing common mistakes helps you avoid many of these mistakes and takes away much of the guesswork. Having rules to abide by helps you avoid these mistakes as well.

Below, I have listed 11 rules that every options day trader must know. Following them is entirely up to you but know that they are proven to help beginner options day trader turn into winning options day traders.

Rule for Success #1 – Have Realistic Expectations

It is sad to say that many people who enter the options trading industry are doing so to make quick money. An option trading is not a get-rich-quick scheme. It is a reputable career that has made many people rich but that is only because these people have put in the time, effort, study and dedication to learning the craft and mastering it. Mastery does not happen overnight and beginner options day traders need to be prepared for that learning curve and to have the fortitude to stick with day trading options even when it becomes tough.

Losses are also part of the game. No trading style or strategy will guarantee gains all the time. In fact, the best options traders have a winning percentage of about 80% and a losing average of approximately 20%. That is why an options day trader needs to be a good money manager and a good risk manager. Be prepared for eventual losses and be prepared to minimize those losses.

Rule for Success #2 – Start Small to Grow a Big Portfolio

Caution is the name of the game when you just get started with day trading options. Remember that you are still learning options trading and developing an understanding of the financial market. Do not jump the gun even if you are eager. After you have practiced paper trading, start with smaller options positions and steadily grow your standing as you get a lay of the options day trading land. This strategy allows you to keep your losses to a minimum and to develop a systematic way of entering positions.

Rule for Success #3 – Know Your Limits

You may be tempted to trade as much as possible to develop a winning monthly average but that strategy will have the opposite effect and land you with a losing average. Remember that every options trader needs careful consideration before that contract is set up. Never overtrade and tie up your investment fund.

Rule for Success #4 – Be Mentally, Physically and Emotionally Prepared Every Day

This is a mentally, physically and emotionally tasking career, and you need to be able to meet the demands of this career. That means keeping your body, mind and heart in good health at all times. Ensure that you schedule time for self-care every day. That can be as simple as taking the time to read for recreation to having elaborate self-care routine carved out in the evenings.

Not keeping your mind, heart and head in optimum health means that they are more likely to fail you. Signs that you need to buckle up and care for yourself more diligently include being constantly tired, being short-tempered, feeling preoccupied, and being easily distracted.

To ensure you perform your best every day, here a few tasks that you need to perform:

- Get the recommended amount of sleep daily. This is between 7 and 9 hours for an adult.

- Practice a balanced diet. The brain and body need adequate nutrition to work their best. Include fruits, complex carbs and veggies in this diet and reduce the consumption of processed foods.

- Eat breakfast lunch and dinner every day. Fuel your mind and body with the main meals. Eating a healthy breakfast is especially important because it helps set the tone for the rest of the day.

- Exercise regularly. Being inactive increases your risk of developing chronic diseases like heart disease, certain cancers and other terrible health consequences. Adding just a few minutes of exercise to your daily routine not only reduces those risks but also allows your brain to function better, which is a huge advantage for an options day trader.

- Drink alcohol in moderation or not at all.

- Stop smoking.

- Reduce stress contributors in your environment.

Rule for Success #5 – Do Your Homework Daily

Get up early and study the financial environment before the market opens and look at the news. This allows you to develop a daily options trading plan. The process of analyzing the financial climate before the market opens is called pre-market preparation. It is a necessary task that needs to be performed every day to asset competition and to align your overall strategy with the short-term conditions of that day.

An easy way to do this is to develop a pre-market checklist. An example of a pre-market checklist includes but is not limited to:

- Checking the individual markets that you frequently trade options in or plan to trade options in to evaluate support and resistance.

- Checking the news to assess whether events that could affect the market developed overnight.

- Assessing what other options traders are doing to determined volume and competition.

- Determining what safe exits for losing positions are.

- Considering the seasonality of certain markets are some as affected by the day of the week, the month of the year, etc.

Rule for Success #6 – Analyze Your Daily Performance

To determine if the options day trading style and strategies that you have adopted are working for you, you need to track your performance. At the most basic, this needs to be done on a daily basis by virtue of the fact that you are trading options daily. This will allow you to notice patterns in your profit and loss. This can lead to you determining the why and how of these gains and losses. These determinations lead to fine tuning your daily processes for maximum returns. These daily performance assessments allow you also to make determinations on the long-term activity of your options day trading career.

Rule for Success #7 – Do Not Be Greedy

If you are fortunate enough to make a 100% return on your investment, do not be greedy and try to reap more benefit from the position. You might have the position turn on you and you can lose everything. When and if such a rare circumstance happens to you, sell your position and take the profits.

Rule for Success #8 – Pay Attention to Volatility

Volatility speaks to how likely a price change will occur over a specific amount of time on the financial market. Volatility can work for an options day trader or against the options day trader. It all depends on what the options day trader is trying to accomplish and what his or her current position is.

There are many external factors that affect volatility and such factors include the economic climate, global events and news reports. Strangles and straddles strategies are great for use in volatile markets.

There are different types of volatility and they include:

- Price volatility, which describes how the price of an asset increases or decreases based on the supply and demand of that asset.

- Historical volatility, which is a measure of how an asset has performed over the last 12 months.

- Implied volatility, which is a measure of how an asset will perform in the future.

Rule for Success #9 – Use the Greeks

Greeks are a collection of measures that provide a gage of an option's price sensitivity in relation to other factors. Each Greek is represented by a letter from the Greek alphabet. These Greeks use complex formulas to be determined but they are the system that option pricing is based on. Even though these calculations can be complex, they can be done quickly and efficiently so that options day traders can use them as a method of advancing their trades for the most profitable position.

Rule for Success #10 – Be Flexible

Many options day traders find it difficult to try trading styles and strategies that they are not familiar with. While the saying of, "Do not fix it if it is not broken," is quite true, you will never become more effective and efficient in this career if you do not step out of your comfort zone at least once in a while. Yes, stick with want work but allow room for the consideration that there may be better alternatives.

Rule for Success #11 – Have an Accountability Partner or Mentorship

Day trading options can be a rather solitary career. That means it becomes easy to sleep in if the urge strikes or just not put in a day of work. While there is nothing wrong with doing that when you have established a solid career in day trading options, this is a slippery slope that can become a harmful habit to your career. Having an accountability partner is an easy way to keep you on track with your trading plan and goals. It keeps you consistent with your actions. This can be a fellow trader, your spouse or romantic partners, a friend or family member.

Finding a mentor is also a great way to incorporate accountability as well as learning in your career.

Conclusion

At every level of options trading, there are mistakes that people do over and over again. However, these mistakes must be avoided in order to realize a profit from the trade.

Just like in stocks trading, you must be able to control your emotions when trading options. Once you have a trading plan, stick to it and do not be quick to exit, no matter how bad things become. To help you achieve this, define your upside and downside exit points in good time. You also need to define the timeframe for your exit, although the trade gives you an opportunity to get out of a call or put option before it expires.

A trade can move against you and make you lose money. Most traders have been there. Sometimes you may put your capital on options, and the outcome is not exactly what you expected. In such a scenario, most traders tend to double up their options strategy to see if they can recover the loss. Doubling may lower your potential for loss in a given trade, but it is surrounded by a lot of risks.

In most cases, it does not work. Most traders who try out this technique end up losing a lot more. Once a loss occurs, it is wise to close the trade and start a different trade to see if you can recover your money.

The stock market is often more liquid than the options market because stock traders focus on one commodity, while options traders often have several contracts to select from. An option quote always has the bid price and the asking price indicated on it. These prices do not indicate the actual value of the option. Illiquidity in options trading may result from illiquid stock. It is, therefore important to trade options that are derived from a highly liquid stock.

Always ensure that you buy back your short strategies in good time. It is important not to assume that a trade will go your way the entire time. This is because trade can change performance in a matter of seconds. In case a short option gets out of the money, and you are able to redeem it then do so before you lose more money in the transaction. One rule of thumb that most traders use is that if you are able to keep 80% of your gain from a sale, then you should buy it back as soon as you can.

Do not allow yourself to learn the lessons the hard way. It is not always wise to attempt a trade while you already know the kind of risks involved. Focus on your trading plan and commit to these tips to succeed in your trade.

If you ever hope to make money trading options successfully, then there are a number of skills that you are going to want to hone as much as possible, starting with the ability to trade like a robot. When you have a trade on the line that could make or break you it is only natural to be scared or anxious, but those emotions are only going to cloud your judgment if left unchecked which is why it so important to box them up and bury them in the ground when you are trading so you can only focus on the facts in front of you. Fail to do so, and you will watch in fear as your sure thing turns into a huge loss as opposed to jumping into action right away in order to salvage as much profit as possible.

Being a successful trader means being able to react at a moment's notice, without hesitation, full stop. The only way you can ever ensure that this is going to be the case is if you can put aside the emotional aspect of what is occurring and focus on the numbers as if it was some else's money. A good way to ensure that this is possible is to make it a point of never putting more on the line then you can afford to lose.

The first emotion you are going to need to learn to banish is anger as it can cloud your judgment without you even realizing it. It is perfectly natural to feel angry when a trade that was going your way suddenly ends up costing your money, that doesn't mean that it is ever the right choice to act on that anger as no good will come of it whatever you might believe at the moment.

Don't always follow the crowd. While doing what the major players in the market do can be a reliable strategy, following the crowd at all times is not advisable in the long-term. Successful traders do their own research and trust themselves enough to act on the results they determine, even if they mean making trades that might seem unpopular at the moment. When it comes to seeking substantial payouts trading against the market is going to be the most likely, if not the most reliable, option. This is only the case if you do so for the right reasons, however, as being contrarian just for the fun of it isn't going to get you any either.

Most of the market movement that takes place each day is caused by sheep who simply follow the crowd with no real idea as to why they are doing what they are doing. Successful traders don't fall into this mindset, however, instead of being a sheep you should strive to be a wolf which means improving your intuition through a combination of practice and diligent study. Eventually, all this hard work will pay off and you will start to become more confident in yourself which will then make it even easier to trust in yourself, and not the sheep, moving forward. It is natural to feel a tinge of fear when you get a signal that your trades are down or if the market as a whole is experiencing a dramatic upheaval. If you don't control this instinct, however, then it can be easy to overreact and find yourself getting rid of your holdings or turtling up and not taking any risks until the perceived crisis has passed. While this will likely lead to fewer losses, it will also negatively affect the potential for additional gains.

In order to bypass this natural reaction, it is important to be aware of what fear really is which is simply a natural reaction to stimuli that can be perceived as a threat. If you find yourself becoming afraid during stressful stock-related scenarios you may find it helpful put the situation into a larger context or to take a moment to consider what it is that you are really afraid of. Either of these exercises will allow you to put the fear on hold and think rationally about the situation which will make it much easier to ignore entirely.

CPSIA information can be obtained
at www.ICGtesting.com
Printed in the USA
LVHW050445161120
671799LV00011B/579